One Soul's Journey

Dear Wilson

It's been a pleasure getting to know you.
I wish you much love & light on your journey.

Best wishes
Linda
7/12/01

One Soul's Journey

Linda Routhier with Maureen Niak

Writers Club Press
San Jose New York Lincoln Shanghai

One Soul's Journey

Writers Club Press
an imprint of iUniverse.com, Inc.

For information address:
iUniverse.com, Inc.
5220 S 16th, Ste. 200
Lincoln, NE 68512
www.iuniverse.com

ISBN: 0-595-12963-3

Printed in the United States of America

To David, forever and always

Linda

ACKNOWLEDGEMENTS

From Linda with love and gratitude to the following people: To my parents, whose steadfast love has given me courage when I couldn't find it on my own. To Pat Cloonen, one of God's messengers, her courage and love of God will live forever. To Carolyn Castel, Judy Donahue, Marie Fricker, Cindi Gigowski, Susan Haigh, Kathy Lofts, Kathy Lea, and Mary Stewart for being kind supporters and reviewers of this book. To Gabriel, Michael, Zechariah, and Jesus for loving us always.

From Maureen: to my spiritual guides and angels without whom this book would not exist—my heartfelt thanks. To the love of my life, for his continued love and understanding, my eternal love. To everyone in my life who has helped me learn the lessons for my soul's growth, I say "Namaste."

INTRODUCTION

I am an ordinary woman who has had some extraordinary experiences. My life has been a roller coaster ride of experiences that Jesus believes you will find enlightening. Why? Because I'm no different from you.

And because I'm no different from you, hopefully you will relate to my story. And, like me, you will discover that you are not alone and that you are loved very much. By God, by Jesus, by Mother Mary, and by your very own team of angels.

I have had to learn, through hardship and heartbreak, that the decisions I made throughout the first forty years of my life were not the most intelligent choices I could have made. I was not the type of wife or mother that other people looked up to but rather the one talked about by those who believed that they were the model wife and mother. Sometimes I wasn't the best of friends, either. But, I really did try. No matter how many times I felt that I had failed, I got back up, brushed myself off and tried again.

And, then miraculously, I began to make the right decisions. I was forced to make changes in my life. And, because of those changes, I slowly re-discovered my spiritual side. I became a healer, a Reiki practitioner, and while Reiki plays a very large part in re-discovering myself and the happy person I knew was bursting to break free, that is not all of the story. I will share with you how I met my soul mate, David. How I was introduced into a more spiritual life. How I met Zechariah, the Archangels Gabriel and Michael, and Jesus. And, how much my life changed because of them.

And, Maureen Niak, my co-author, without whom I would never have been introduced to one of the best friends anyone could ask for. For it was through Maureen's ability to channel Jesus and the others who wished to speak to me that my life changed completely.

Come share with me a journey of discovery…of hope…and of love.

Linda Routhier

Note: All events in this book are true. Some names have been changed.

So now I am giving you a new commandment: Love each other. Just as I have loved you, you should love each other.

Jesus to his disciples at The Last Supper
John 14:34

PART ONE

I Asked For...

I asked God for strength that I might achieve.
I was made weak that I might learn humbly to obey.
I asked for health that I might do greater things.
I was given infirmity that I might do better things.
I asked for riches that I might be happy.
I was given poverty that I might be wise.
I asked for power that I might have the praise of others.
I was given weakness that I might feel the need of God.
I asked for all things that I might enjoy all things.
I was given life that I might enjoy all things.
I got nothing I asked for, but everything I hoped for.
Almost despite myself, my unspoken prayers were answered.
I am, among all people, most richly blessed.

Unknown

IN THE BEGINNING

I was born in November 1953 to a young married couple who were very much in love. I loved my parents and felt loved and protected in return. My father was considered very handsome, a policeman who looked just like Lloyd Bridges during his *Seahunt* days. My mother was a very pretty housewife whom I adored. As the years passed, my two brothers and two sisters joined the family. My brother and I, as the two oldest, seldom left my mother's side. Mother likes to tell people how, when we were small, my brother and I would tell her that we were going to come back [in our next lifetime] as ashtrays. That way, we would always be with her because wherever she went she always carried an ashtray.

I remember when my first sister was born. My baby brother and I were staying with my father's parents while my mother was in the hospital. It was the day before Easter and, being four years old, I was worried that the Easter Bunny wouldn't find us because we weren't home. Dad and my grandparents tried to reassure me but I had my doubts. When I woke up Easter Sunday morning, loving the thrill of anticipation, I slowly made my way into the living room. To my delight and great relief, there were Easter baskets full of goodies waiting for my brother and me. Giving us hugs and kisses, my dad told us that the best Easter present was from God. He had given us a new baby sister. Having a new sister was nice but all I really cared about that morning was the candy in my Easter basket.

On the day I turned eight, my younger sister was almost born! But, mom's labor continued past midnight so my sister was actually born the next day. I was disappointed because I thought it would be great to have a sister with the same birthday as me. Looking back over the years, it was as if they were the same because our birthdays were always celebrated together.

When I was twelve, my youngest brother was born; but I'm getting ahead of myself. Suffice it to say that there were a total of five children in my family with myself the oldest. We were sometimes mischievous children but otherwise good kids. We were a happy family—or so I thought.

We lived in an apartment in Brookline, just outside of Boston, for my formative years. We had a happy normal life until one day, my father moved out. I was ten years old and will always remember him coming to visit and telling me that he would always love us no matter what happened. He had come to take us children out for the day. When we returned home, dad didn't come into the house but as we stood beside his car he hugged me, kissed me and told me how much he loved me. Then, I led my brother and sisters into the building we lived in, waving goodbye to daddy just before we went inside. I was too young to know what the problem with my parents was but could see that they were both very unhappy. Mom cried a lot and dad always looked sad. My brother, sisters and I felt confused and scared. What was going to happen to us now?

As time went on, we all became accustomed to the new order in our lives. We lived with mom in the same apartment in the projects that we always had. Dad came and took us out every Sunday. I had the same friends, playmates and enemies that I had always had. But, our lives had changed and I didn't like the changes. I wanted my daddy home where he belonged. I hated kissing him goodbye. I wanted him to kiss me goodnight when I went to bed at night and to fix my breakfast in the morning. As wonderful as visiting my grandparent's house was, it wasn't home and home was where I felt my daddy belonged. But, he never came home again. He only came to take us out for the day.

Looking back, I don't remember being poor but apparently there wasn't much money to go around or we wouldn't have been living in the projects. I do remember playing a lot, going to the parks and playing games with the Park Teachers and my friends. I was ten, my brother was eight, and my sisters were six and two. Mom must have felt overwhelmed trying to care for us on her own. I can remember once when all four of us children got the German measles at the same time. That was very difficult for Mom, as it would be for anyone. Being the oldest, I grew up a bit faster than most kids to help my mom care for the family. Sometimes I felt overwhelmed and would cry at the unfairness of it all. I wanted my happy home back.

I did get to go to camp, though. The Rotary Club sent me the first year and then my brother and I got to go the second year. I didn't know that we were poor and that sending us to camp was the Rotarian's contribution to those less financially fortunate than they. All I knew was that I was going to camp for two weeks. Yahoo! I couldn't wait to go.

Getting on school buses in the Village, we headed off on what I was sure to be a great adventure. The bus stopped in Charlestown and we got very nervous. This didn't look like a camp to any of us sitting on the bus. The driver calmed our fears though by telling us that we were picking up additional children. Oh. Whew, that was a relief. More kids could only be a good thing. A black girl sat next to me and we talked all the way to camp. When we got there and were assigned to cabins, I was relieved that my new friend and I were assigned to the same one. I had never known a black person so I had a lot of questions for her. Never having been exposed to any type of prejudice, I wasn't aware that she might have been uncomfortable with all my questions about her skin. I can't remember her name but will always remember how envious I was of her naturally dark skin. *She* didn't have to worry about getting sunburned the way I did. I thought it must be wonderful to have a year round tan. Despite all the sunburn medication I was constantly rubbing into my skin, I had a wonderful two weeks. Then it was time to go home. My friend and I had to say farewell and we found that to be incredibly difficult. We both had tears running down our cheeks as we waved goodbye to each other. We never saw each other again but I never forgot her. I wonder if she still remembers me, and all the questions that blonde, pasty-skinned white girl asked?

Mom's best friend, Madeline, was my godmother. Madeline was a professional model, very beautiful and glamorous. She was very tall, slender and had shoulder length, shiny, dark brown hair. Madeline had a wonderful sense of humor and could always make me laugh.

To ease the unhappiness I felt, Madeline enrolled me in charm school at a large department store in Boston. To my delight, for three months or so, every Saturday morning Madeline would bring me into Boston. While charm school was fun, the best part was spending the rest of the day with Madeline. We went to fancy restaurants for lunch and I would drink Shirley Temples. I was introduced to a life beyond my wildest dreams and loved every minute of it. Sometimes, we went to the movies, also. We saw *Mary Poppins, The Sound of Music* and *My Fair Lady* on our excursions. Not only did my godmother treat me like a princess (and sometimes had me dress in frilly dresses that I hated), for one day a week, I had someone's love and attention all to myself. And, that was the best part of all!

To make the wonderful weekends complete, I saw dad on Sunday. Of course, my brother and sisters were there, too but after having the day before with Madeline, I didn't mind.

After a couple of years, my mother fell in love with Jack, a man who appeared to be very nice. Jack was an attractive man with dark hair and blue eyes, was tall and solidly built. He did all the right things to get along with us kids. My mother said we loved him and were glad he was in our lives. I don't ever remember feeling that way. I think we liked him well enough so that everyone got along and my mom, feeling comfortable and reassured, married him. We were to spend the weekend of the wedding with my cousins. We didn't know that mom and Jack weren't married before this and our cousins took great delight in telling us that not only was there going to be a marriage starring our mother but that we were to be kept out of the way during the wedding and honeymoon. I can understand not being told. After all it was 1964 and men and women did not live together without the benefit of marriage. How could my mother tell us girls that we couldn't have sex without marriage and she was doing it! But, at the time, we were puzzled that we weren't invited to the wedding. We never made the connection my mother was worried about.

On the plus side, I was going to be part of a normal family again! A *real* family with a mother, a father and brothers and sisters, just as my friends did. Hooray! Shortly after the wedding, I asked my mother if we would call Jack "dad" instead of by his name. Mom said no because we already had a dad. I knew that but didn't have the heart to tell her that it wasn't because I loved my new stepfather that I asked. It was because I didn't want to look different from any other family. It was humiliating for my name to be different from my mother's and to call my stepfather by his first name when other kids called their fathers "dad." And, talk about how confused my young friends were when addressing my mother. Sometimes they called her Mrs. Green but then got confused knowing that was wrong.

Laughing, mom would say, "Just call me Frank! Now, isn't that easier?"

The humor mom used did alleviate some of my humiliation but I hated being different. Kids pick on you when you're different. And, pick on us, they did. We learned to defend ourselves and after winning a few fights we were left alone.

I was very competitive and played on the Park's softball and kickball teams. I was good too, one of the best players on the team. I found that I excelled in sports of any kind. To me there was nothing better than competing and winning. Whether I was fighting to defend my younger brother and sisters or to defend myself, I had to win. By the time I was twelve, the other kids in the park or in the projects knew better than to get in my way. I fought and played hard and after winning a fight with one of the older girls I was left alone. It's a good thing too because mom was threatening to do bodily harm if I ruined one more dress due to fighting.

A few months after the wedding, life began to change in our house. In some ways our life was better but it took adulthood to see it. There was more money in the house as we did move out of the projects into a nice apartment and then again into a nice suburban home. As far as my siblings and I were concerned life became hell. Our new stepfather was not the nice man he first appeared to be and, as many a newlywed has found, the "real" person comes out after the wedding.

Many a time, I would think about Cinderella and considered myself a modern day version of that fairy tale lady. My mother was often ill with various physical maladies so it was up to me to take care of my brothers and sisters, keep our home neat and clean and I learned to cook. It wasn't long before I could put an entire Sunday dinner on the table. Then my youngest brother was born. He was so cute! I loved helping to take care of him and playing with him. Though, when taking care of him became my full time job after school, I resented that! So, now there were five of us.

The house could get pretty loud with the fighting and playing that go along with a house full of kids. We were very close. When one of us was punished, the other four huddled together waiting to comfort the hurt one. It went far to bond us and we all truly loved each other, no matter how often we fought. When one of us became ill enough to have to stay in bed, the others took turns bringing food and drinks, being company, and playing games. When we were all healthy, a good wrestling match or tickle fight were favorite ways to blow off steam.

Except for Sunday dinner, Jack never bothered to eat dinner with us. I imagine my mother forced him to join us in the dining room because Sunday dinner was always an event for mom. The balance of the week he ate in the living room watching television while the rest of the family had supper in the kitchen. When mom was in a bad mood the five of us were expected to be silent. We couldn't do it. No matter how much we loved our mother or how good we wanted to be, it was too much to ask for five children to be silent for an entire meal. While my mother ignored us, we would steal looks at her and at each other. Inevitably, one of us would start giggling. That would set the others off. Glaring, mom would sharply tell us to be quiet. We tried but it always had the opposite effect. Once we knew that we had gotten to her, the five of us would be in gales laughing. Trying to be stern and get some semblance of order back in her kitchen, the offending giggler would be sent to finish eating in the dining room. Another mistake. Out of mom's sight, behind the closed dining room door, the offender would no longer feel compelled to comply with my mother's order to be silent. Uncontrolled laughter from the dining room could be heard in the kitchen. Surrendering, mom would join in the fun and the offender was then singled out as the tickle victim. Not liking being the victim I quickly learned not to be ticklish. My youngest sister never learned that trick and, being very ticklish, was frequently the victim. The rules of the game: the victim was caught, wrestled to the floor and tickled until the family dog joined in the fun by licking the victim's face until the victim had tears of laughter streaming down her face. But, it was always great fun when my mother was the tickle victim. And, no matter what had originally caused my mother's bad mood, it was always dispelled by a good tickle fight.

One afternoon when I was thirteen, while bathing, the bathroom door flew open and Jack stormed in, yelling at me. He hauled me out of the tub and dragged me, dripping and naked, out into the kitchen. While I stood there trying to cover myself with my hands, he held up a dirty glass that I had washed and put away. Jack was yelling at me for putting away unclean dishes and then, with the dirty glass, struck me on my forehead breaking the glass. Having vented, he stormed out of the kitchen, leaving me standing there in shock.

After Jack left the kitchen, I cleaned up the broken glass so none of my younger brothers or sisters would get cut. Then, I went back into the bathroom, closed the door and looked in the mirror, horrified that I had so much blood on me. Shaking, I stood there washing the blood off my face and neck. Fortunately, it was only a small nick. That done, I sat on the side of the bathtub trying to absorb what had just happened to me. Nothing in my thirteen years had prepared me for such treatment. I dressed, and after making sure that my stepfather had left the apartment, I told my mother what had happened. She hugged me and held me and told me that she loved me and would never let anything like that happen again. Naturally, I felt loved and protected. Mom could be fierce when it came to us kids and I trusted that. I never heard what she said to him but Jack never again barged in on me when I was behind closed doors.

I had my small revenges over the years. Being naturally sarcastic and having the inability to hide my feelings kept me in trouble with Jack. I could no more keep the dirty looks off my face or the sarcastic replies from passing my lips than I could learn to like my stepfather. I hated him with a passion that kept me awake nights.

Naturally, every dirty look or wisecrack earned punishment. Apparently my hatred was greater than my fear. While I never learned to control my facial muscles or to keep my mouth shut, I did learn how to aggravate him in ways that earned no punishment. I simply pretended to be a slow moving airhead when he told me to do something. I hated doing anything for him so if he made the mistake of sending me upstairs to perform a task I slowly made my way up the stairs. Reaching the top I would turn around and slowly make my way back down. When Jack was in sight I would pretend to look shamefaced and ask, "What did you want again? I forget". Got him every time. It made him crazy but was not a punishable offense. I earned the nickname "Flash" because I moved so slowly. I considered it a small price to pay for my little victories. No wonder I won all the fights I got in. I had quite a bit of rage locked inside my adolescent body.

The abuse never stopped as long as we lived in the same house with Jack. Any one of my siblings could tell their own tales. Let's just say that every one of us moved out of the house as soon as college started and none of us ever moved back in. My purpose in documenting these stories is not to detail an unhappy adolescence but to point out that it was unhappy and as you will see, my angels did try to help me. Of course, I never made the connection until many years later.

THE TEEN YEARS

Growing up a good Irish Catholic girl I went to church every Sunday, followed by Sunday school. I learned my catechism and made my First Communion. For the most part, I was considered a "good" girl. What the nuns didn't know however was that I had a nightly visitor.

When I was twelve, my family moved to a new apartment, across the street from the projects where I grew up. My two sisters and I shared a regular sized bedroom, with me in the top bunk. The beds were set up so that our heads were to the rear of the bedroom while our feet faced the door. Late one night, for some inexplicable reason, I woke up and saw the shadow of a man standing just outside my bedroom door. I didn't know who it was and, of course, I was frightened. I pulled the blankets over my head and ever so slowly, peeked out and saw that he was still there in the same position. Again, I pulled the blankets over my head and peeked out but he hadn't moved. I did this several times and saw that he remained in the same place each time. After some time had passed, I felt reassured enough to go back to sleep. Looking back now, I wonder why I didn't scream or call out for my mother. Perhaps because the shadow didn't move, never approached, never spoke, just stayed outside the doorway.

After that first sighting, as I saw him night after night, I was soothed by his presence. My mother and I had no idea who it could be but guessed that it could be her father watching over me. It made sense to us as my mother is the baby of her family and I am the oldest child in my family. And, he did seem directed at me, as my younger sisters were never aware of him. As time went by, I would wake up just to make sure he was there. And, he was—for the next two years.

From the time I was twelve until after I turned eighteen, I had blackouts. This did not mean I fell down because I didn't. I would be playing in a softball game, for instance. Suddenly people were standing in front of me asking if I was okay. Apparently, I had just stood there, not moving or blinking for a few minutes then I would blink and all these people would excitedly be asking if I was alright. It was frightening to me. I had no recollection of blacking out but to blink and see all those people talking at me was scary. For me, no time had passed and I couldn't understand how people had been able to approach without my seeing them. I generally took a step back in shock. I had no explanation but clearly there was something wrong with me. Since the adults in my life needed an explanation, I was diagnosed with Petit Mal, a mild form of Epilepsy. And, as predicted by the doctors, the blackouts ended when I was eighteen.

When it was time for my Confirmation, I had to choose a name that would become part of me forever. The only rule in choosing a name was that it had to be a biblical name, preferably a saint's name. The name I chose was Madeline, after my godmother, whom I loved with all my heart. This really sent the nuns into a tizzy because my middle name is Mary. By taking Madeline as my Confirmation name, the Church would see my name as Linda Mary Magdalene. The name sounded wonderful to me but Sister Mary Margaret was very upset and refused to allow me my choice. I was told to select another name, one more suitable for a young girl. Confused and heartbroken I came home from Sunday school crying. Sobbing, I told my mom what had taken place. She was incensed to think that a nun would put such ideas into my head and contacted Monsignor Robinson. After many debates, I was allowed to keep the name Madeline. When the big moment came and my new full name was announced, I felt so proud. Who knows what my Confirmation name would have been if my mother hadn't fiercely defended my right to choose the name I wanted. If you ask me, Linda Mary Madeline sounds just fine!

Recently, I asked my mother what Madeline had thought of all the commotion and was told that she thought it was a hoot! She was very touched, though, that I wanted to take her name as part of mine.

When I was a fourteen year-old freshman in high school, my family moved to a new house in a suburban town. While I loved the fact that I was finally allowed to have my own room, the room did not allow a direct view into the hallway. I thought that my nightly friend was gone because I could no longer see him. I was wrong though. For the next ten years I would hear him speak to me, usually the sound was only heard in my right ear. Often he only called my name and other times he spoke a sentence, but always as a forewarning. Over time, I learned that when I heard my name called, it always prefaced a bit of trouble. This presence was a major part of my life until I reached my mid-twenties. But, it was many years later before I learned who he is.

I hated my new high school and everything about it. I went from knowing everyone and being popular to being the new kid in school. Because I was an unknown I was a non-entity. The only people I knew were the girls my age in the neighborhood. Nice girls, I liked them and looked forward to the ritual of Ellen, Val and me trying to get Olga ready for school because she was always late and we couldn't leave without her. My new friends had brothers, younger and older, so we made up quite a friendly neighborhood. The girls worked hard to help me adjust to the new school system but it just wasn't the same and I missed my old neighborhood and friends. One thing that earned me some notoriety in my new school was my ability to fight. One of the girls in my gym class called me out for a fight after school. I don't remember why but the small spark of a memory tells me that it was for something stupid. But then again aren't most fights? At the end of the day when I walked out of school there was the bully standing waiting for me, with a crowd standing and waiting for the outcome. I won the fight in short order and while she never became a friend of mine, other people took notice and I began to make more friends. But Ellen was my best friend and remained so all throughout high school.

I wasn't very pretty or stylish nor did I wear any makeup until my senior year. I also had little fun, was never invited to parties and never had a boyfriend. Life at school was no fun, life at home was worse. The '60's might have been great for some people but I needed the '70's to blossom. And, like the ugly duckling I turned into a swan. You could say that I was a late bloomer. My still blonde hair had gotten longer, I lost baby fat, put makeup on and my hemline rose from the middle of my shins to midthigh. During my transformation I was introduced to Richie by another friend of mine. Richie became my high school sweetheart. Having now blossomed, the other boys in school noticed me. One male friend suggested that I dump Richie because he knew of other boys who wanted to ask me out. My attitude was Richie accepted me for who I was before the other boys noticed me and I was staying with my boyfriend. The others could go jump in a lake. I wasn't interested. Strangely enough that earned me even more respect and the "popular" people took notice of me.

Near the end of senior year one of the classes I attended planned to enter a regional district contest. Everyone in class had to participate. Not being the least artistically inclined and having no interest in creating shadowboxes, I agreed to enter the Miss Sweetheart contest. On the day of the contest, having no doubt that I didn't stand a chance I sat before a panel of judges while they asked questions and I answered. At the end of the day when my name was announced as first runner-up I didn't hear it. My teacher had to give me a nudge to move onto the stage. In shock I joined the other runners-up while the winner's name was called. My high school stock rose quite a bit the next day when the principal announced all the contest winner's names over the public address system.

The only other claim to fame I had during senior year was my love of debating another student in Civics class. The debate was not a formal process. I simply opposed everything another girl stood for and couldn't keep my mouth shut whenever she stated her opinion. I think she enjoyed the debates as much as I did. Certainly the other students did because once we started nothing else was accomplished. Apparently our teacher enjoyed it quite a bit as well.

Between being Miss Sweetheart and Civics debater my senior year ended with a bang. I was invited to parties, had lots of fun with Richie and Ellen, and was feeling good about life. Even my existence at home was tolerable. I wasn't around enough to get into much trouble. I worked in a clothing store at the mall after school and nights, had homework, dates and my parents could not complain about my grades. I graduated with good grades but not the honor roll. As bad as my high school career had started, it had a great ending.

In 1971, at seventeen, I went away to college and left Richie and my Catholic neighborhood behind. For the first time in my young life, I was free! I met people of various faiths, beliefs and backgrounds. There were many Vietnam veterans in attendance, as well. I was fascinated with the Baptists and Judaism and wanted to learn more. Looking back now, I don't remember how I came to the conclusion that confession (in my young and very arrogant opinion) was an unnecessary Catholic rite. I do remember telling my mother that I would no longer go to confession. It bothered me that my mother was a devout Catholic, but the church had excommunicated her because she was divorced. Mom grew up in a convent and that her deep religious convictions could be tossed aside by the church angered us all. It seemed to me that the church should be happy to have as many people attending Mass as they could get. We argued for a while and I agreed to go to confession one more time to make her happy.

I entered the confessional, knelt before the screen, made the sign of the cross and said "Bless me, Father, for I have sinned," and stopped. I had nothing more to say. I simply couldn't compromise my belief that I didn't need an intermediary between God and myself. If everything that I learned in Sunday school was true, that God was everywhere and knew everything that we did, why did I need to come to Church and abase myself by having another person know my sins? I didn't believe that all of my sins would be forgiven if I said three Hail Mary's and four Our Fathers. I simply didn't buy it. Fortunately for me, a new priest, Father Mike, had joined the parish and was on the other side of the screen. In response to my silence, he asked what was wrong. Blushing, I told him that my sins were none of his business. Surprised, he asked why I had come and was quite understanding when I told him that I came to please my mother.

The priest and I left the confessional, sat in a pew and talked about the situation. Father Mike asked if I was sorry for my sins and I admitted that I was. Then added that since I knew that God had already forgiven me for my sins and *He* didn't require that I say my Hail Mary's and Our Fathers, why should the Church? I don't remember his answer to that question. I do remember his kindness and understanding, though. I was very grateful that young Father Mike was on duty that long ago Saturday afternoon, and not one of the older priests! I may not remember what he looked like, but I will never forget him. I was still given several Our Father's and Hail Mary's to pray at the altar, which I did, but those prayers didn't have much meaning for me at the time. It was a very hollow victory.

My mother was mortified when I came home and told her of my ill-fated confession. She never asked me to attend confession again. We did agree on one thing, though. I acknowledged that priests were very important and necessary—there was no argument from me there, but I have never changed my mind about confession.

A short time later, I failed at college life. Some would say that I had too much freedom too fast. That could be true. Never having had any freedom I thoroughly enjoyed having so much. Perhaps I went a little overboard. Okay, I went way overboard! I discovered everything at once: boys, alcohol and drugs and not one person to tell me that I couldn't do or have whatever I wanted, whenever I wanted it. It was heady, this freedom I had. I reveled in it. I drank too much, did too many drugs, had unprotected sex and a wonderful time for myself. Of course, such a lifestyle is not conducive to good grades but I didn't care. I was having unlimited fun. Amazing that I managed to have religious discussions and experiences living the life I was but I managed to be sober occasionally.

Something (I really don't remember what) happened in my life back then that caused me to have a panic attack and I was given tranquilizers to prevent further attacks. As I was preparing to take my midterms, I was stressed because I was not as prepared as I should be (the night before was a late one). I took several tranquilizers figuring the more I took the faster they would work. It was an incredibly stupid thing to do. I nearly died of a drug overdose. The paramedics came and performing CPR, helped me to breathe again. I remember looking down at the scene and hearing a paramedic ask a girl friend if I was wearing a bra. My friend indignantly wanted to know why he asked. He replied that if I had a bra on, then he could open my dress to perform the CPR. Well, it was 1971 and not many young women were wearing bras back then. Including me. The paramedics had to make do. The next thing I remembered, I was being wheeled into an ambulance and on my way to the hospital. It was years later when I realized that my watching the paramedics give me CPR was an actual out-of-body experience.

No one could figure out what was wrong with me. After almost two weeks of having every test the doctor's could think of, they were stumped and so was I. Near the end of my second week in the hospital, a neurosurgeon asked if I had been taking any prescriptions. (Amazing that no one had thought to ask that question sooner.)

"Why, yes," I replied and reached into the bed table drawer. As I held the prescription bottle in my hand I knew what had happened to me.

The doctor took pity on me, and my ignorance, and I was released from the hospital the next day, embarrassed but no longer ignorant about taking medications.

I was stupid in so many other ways but it all boils down to the fact that I wanted to feel loved and accepted, and was willing to do whatever it took to get what I wanted. I became pregnant. Fortunately, I knew who the father was as I had for a short time, been steadily dating one fellow. Unfortunately, we were no longer together and could no longer stand each other. It wasn't pretty when I went home for the Thanksgiving holiday.

Being a coward and fearful of my mother's reaction to my pregnancy, I delayed sharing my news until shortly before the holiday weekend was over. I had no choice but to tell her about the pregnancy. She was very angry when I told her of my condition and that I planned to keep the baby and, no, I would not marry the father nor would I tell anyone his name. I was grateful when she finally accepted the situation. We spent the afternoon making plans for the baby and spoke of my leaving school and getting a job to prepare to support my child.

That evening, after mom gave the news to Jack, I was called in to their bedroom for a talk. The talk was about the need for me to have an abortion. I didn't want one! I was given a choice to either have an abortion or get married. My parents winning argument: how could they tell my younger sisters that they shouldn't have sex before marriage while I was planning to be a single mother? (Perhaps it is a good thing I didn't know that *they* had lived together without benefit of marriage.)

I allowed myself to be persuaded to have the abortion, telling myself that my parents were right. I didn't want my sisters to be in the same predicament that I had gotten myself into. At the same time, I wanted to have my baby but couldn't go against the family. Nor could I forgive myself for making that decision until I realized, many years later, that God had seen my pain and had already forgiven me. Only then could I learn to forgive myself.

To give my mother and stepfather credit, they said they would never discuss the abortion, never throw it in my face and they never did.

I learned a lifelong lesson during my college days. I learned not to judge people as harshly as I had in the past. Like most kids, everyone and everything I saw was seen in black and white.

There was a boy who was a good friend. He had the greatest name, Mesislaus Thaddeus Bryzinski. I just loved that name—never forgot it. We called him Mickey.

As I said, Mickey was a good friend. He was quiet and kept to himself but was generous when with others. I never heard him say a bad word about anyone.

I was horrified to hear someone call him a very bad name. I was very upset and couldn't understand why everyone didn't see what a good person Mickey was. I had to give this situation a lot of thought because no matter how much I liked Mickey, others are entitled to their own opinion. Being the Vietnam era, I was well aware that one of our countries greatest human rights is based upon freedom of speech. I felt I couldn't say or do anything to defend my friend. This was too new a revelation for me to say anything or act quickly in his defense.

I thought about this situation for many days before coming to a decision. The next time I heard someone say something against a person I cared about, I would not keep silent, nor would I make anyone feel less for stating their opinion. If I could not rationally change the opinion, I would agree to disagree with that person. I felt that showed love and respect to all involved.

This was, in my mind, the first adult decision I had ever made and it felt good and right and just.

JESUS FREAKS

After the abortion, I was still unforgiving of myself and rebelled against my mother and stepfather. I couldn't forgive them for their part in my having an abortion. It was the straw that broke this camel's back. I ran away and refused to ever live in that house again. It was decided that I would move in with my father. I never returned to college.

I was ready to make some serious changes in my life. Dad did not know of my disgrace which helped to make our lives together wonderful. I truly loved my father and loved living with him. I felt no stress because we had a very comfortable relationship. I was beginning to heal. After a few months with my father, the blackouts stopped.

Eventually, I met the two young men in the apartment next to ours. Thanks to my new neighbors I was introduced to a group of people my age or slightly older and they took me under their wings. Nowadays, I understand they are called Born Again Christians but back in the early 1970's, we were called Jesus Freaks. I was 18 years old and starving for something I could believe in and still looking for love and acceptance. I wholeheartedly threw myself into my new life. I was given a bible; attended bible studies, and became a "good" *Christian* girl. My new friends and I tried very hard to live our lives according to the bible. And, instead of doing drugs, we worked to help others get off drugs.

I was happy with my new life and welcomed the changes I was experiencing. After a while, things began to happen that couldn't be explained. During a bible study, sitting across from Dave, who was leading the study, I noticed a pale yellow glow around him. At first, I thought the glow was from the lamp placed next to him but realized that it couldn't be. The shade of the lamp cast him in a conical shaped light, while the glow I saw was larger than the lamplight. I pointed to the glow and asked those sitting beside me if they could see it. They couldn't. No one believed me which only made me stubborn and out to prove that I wasn't seeing things. But, no matter what I did, it was obvious to one and all that there was something wrong with my eyes for they believed it was not possible for me to see something they couldn't.

Shortly after this, my new friends and I went to the beach where we were approached by several Jehovah's Witnesses. A lively biblical conversation ensued and much to everyone's surprise, I began quoting the bible and making sense, too! What made it surprising was that while I had read parts of the bible, I hadn't yet memorized anything from it. Nonetheless here I was, trading scripture for scripture with people who knew the bible inside out. When we moved along, my friends asked how I did it, but I had no explanation. And, later on that afternoon, I could not repeat the bible quotes that I had stated earlier. Still, none of us thought too much of it until a spectacular event happened and my friends began to look at me differently.

During bible study several weeks later, I had the strongest feeling that we should link hands. I couldn't explain the feeling or where it had come from, I just knew that we had to do it. Fortunately, with a shrug that said why not, everyone went along with my crazy idea. While sitting on the floor, we joined hands forming a circle.

Suddenly, we were basked in a bright yellow-white light and while I don't remember seeing anyone, I knew that we were not alone. The light was coming from behind me and radiated out to envelop all of us. We were so caught up in the feeling of love and joy emanating from the light that we began to laugh. We felt suffused with happiness. The light didn't last long, perhaps a minute but in that moment, we knew that we were loved and that God was smiling down upon us.

When the light faded and the laughter came to an end, we looked at each other in wonder. We were awestruck by what had just transpired. Though none could explain what had happened to us, one thing was certain, somehow I was the cause of it. My friends knew it and I knew it. My ability to see auras and quote from the bible was remembered and suddenly I was "special." And, I loved feeling special. It felt wonderful.

And this miraculous event happened even though I had been wicked in the previous few years. I had slept around, had drunk too much, done drugs, had an abortion, been a wild child and still found my way back to God and He smiled down upon me.

It was many years later when I learned the identity of this night's visitor. It was an event never to be forgotten.

Metaphysically, things were really heating up for me after that night. I was becoming more clairvoyant, dreams were coming true and, some of those dreams occurred while I was awake. I saw auras around people all the time; knew when the telephone was about to ring, who was calling and why. Best of all, I still heard my old friend speak in my right ear.

There was one man in our merry band that I had become attracted to. His name was Bill and I thought him so handsome with long, straight, lustrous dark hair and brown eyes, full beard and mustache. He was tall, well built and liked to laugh. I was thrilled the day he asked me out on our first date. I thought we made a striking couple–he with his dark Italian looks, me with my fair Irish skin and blonde hair.

One date turned into many and we became an established couple. The one bone of contention between us was the fact that he didn't like what was beginning to happen within our circle of friends. Bill was very street smart but I was still naïve about people. He felt that a shift had taken place due to newer member's attitudes but I didn't see it.

As time passed however, just as Bill had become, I too was becoming disenchanted with the people I was involved with. It took me longer to realize that life and people weren't always as they appeared but eventually I did. I had considered my friends and myself as a cut above the rest.

In my mind, living according to the bible meant that we didn't lie, cheat, backstab or gossip but treated everyone with love and respect. I began to see that this wasn't always true. Disenchanted, Bill and I left the group.

Eventually, forgetting the spectacular events, I also left God.

LIFE WITH BILL

I was madly in love with Bill and he loved me right back. We were two lost souls looking for love and found it in each other. He introduced me to his parents and brother. We all got along wonderfully and I became a frequent visitor. My dad was working as a truck driver and would sometimes have to be out on the road overnight. I didn't like being alone and eventually the guest room at Bill's parent's house became my room when dad was on the road. I was grateful for an alternate place to stay but I really loved spending extra time with Bill.

When Bill came to my family's house he had a difficult time with how rambunctious we were. He was shocked to discover that we were allowed to play and wrestle in the house. We couldn't believe he and his brother weren't allowed to play in their house. So, feeling sorry for him, we taught him how to wrestle in the house—we never broke anything— amazing Bill. After a while, he really got into it. I think it was secretly a guilty pleasure for him. We just loved the fact that he was having fun. When we announced our engagement both families were happy for us.

Shortly before our marriage, as he was cleaning out his bedroom in preparation for the move to our new apartment, he came across his bible. And, before my horrified eyes, he began ripping the pages out of the book. I tried to stop him but was unable to and, with tears in my eyes, watched him destroy what had previously been one of his most prized possessions.

We were young. I was nineteen and he was twenty-one. Almost from the beginning, we were a failure as a married couple. I was still madly in love with him but he didn't like being married. After three months of marriage, we were planning to split up. The day before the planned breakup we were in a terrible car accident. I was a mess and in the hospital for three weeks recovering from internal injuries, pelvic fractures and assorted cuts and abrasions. When the time came for me to go home, I didn't want to. I wasn't sure where I would be going, didn't know if I was going home or even where home was. And, then I had to get past my terror of being in a car again. While intellectually I knew the accident wasn't my husband's fault (we had been run off the road on a hairpin turn), I wasn't recovered enough to brave another accident. Not having yet replaced the car that was totaled, friends drove us home. We were in the backseat and I kept my face buried in Bill's chest with my eyes closed for the entire ride. To my great relief, we made it home in one piece. Using a walker I slowly made my way into the home I hadn't expected to see again.

As if the accident reminded us as to why we had gotten married in the first place, we worked hard to make the marriage work. Having been in the hospital for so long, I was not using birth control and immediately became pregnant. Because my injured pelvis wasn't strong enough to bear any additional weight, I lost the baby. Two weeks after the D&C I became pregnant again. Amazingly, I knew the moment I conceived. As we lay together, basking in the afterglow, I turned to Bill and announced that we were going to have a baby. Bill thought I was crazy and didn't believe me. I had no doubts, though and felt quite smug when the doctor confirmed my pregnancy.

This time, my very determined daughter, Lisa, was born. I felt as if she had worked very hard to be with us. She had been breach and forceps were needed to deliver her. Remarkably, there were no marks on her to show the difficult time she had. Lisa was beautiful with Bill's olive toned skin and my blonde hair and blue eyes. Knowing that most Caucasian babies are born with blue eyes, we didn't know if her eyes would turn brown like Bill's or become hazel like mine. Today, she has beautiful green eyes. Unfortunately, while my husband and I were totally in love with our daughter, it wasn't enough to keep us together as a family. I was devastated when our marriage ended because I truly loved my husband and wanted the marriage to work. But he didn't feel the same. He felt too young to be trapped by a wife and child and all the responsibility that goes along with it.

I knew that it didn't matter how much I loved him, it was just as important that he love and respect me in return. I refused to live with an abusive husband and he was beginning to become that way. Uh, uh. No way. Not me. I had had my share of beatings growing up and had no intention of allowing anyone to beat me ever again. After two years of marriage, I made him leave. I told him that when he could prove that he loved and respected me, he could come home. But he never did. He liked having his freedom.

My marriage did nothing to keep me feeling close to God. I don't remember thinking of Him very often, unless I was in trouble or afraid. I hadn't completely left Him yet, but He was no longer a part of everything I did. I was very angry and hurt by the failure of my marriage. All I had wanted out of life was to be a wife and mother because they are loved so much. Here I was, at twenty-one, a single mother forced to accept Welfare. It was galling. Life certainly wasn't turning out the way I expected it to. On the plus side, I had Lisa who was the joy in my life. For the first time, someone truly loved me and I adored her in return. Only in hindsight could I see how much I was changed by the birth of my daughter. As my marriage fell apart, and my love rejected by my husband, Lisa became the focus of my life. Being a baby she could make me laugh the way no one else ever could. I was a success as a mother. At last I was a success at something.

When my daughter was a year old, I was in another car accident. I was trapped inside a burning car and rescued by one of the other passengers. When he realized that I couldn't run away from the car, he half carried and half dragged me away from the car. Fortunately, the car didn't explode but I suffered not only a broken my hip but had once again fractured my pelvis. Another long and difficult convalescence ensued.

Having now cheated death three times I had lots of time to think about the meaning of life. I sensed that there had to be a reason that I was alive but I couldn't imagine why. Seeing Lisa through life was the most likely answer I could come up with. That answer didn't feel right, however. I still felt that something was missing.

Since I couldn't define a reason for my life, I decided that there was no purpose to it. Somehow, we were born, lived and then died. I convinced myself that there was no such thing as heaven and that hell was the life we were all living. There was nothing more. I turned my back on God and became an agnostic.

Being a single mother, it was difficult making ends meet. When Lisa was two, I got a job working as a bartender at night. I had never made an alcoholic drink before but the owner was desperate and I was young and pretty so I got the job. I learned to mix drinks and pour a beer. I also learned to have fun again. I made many friends during the three years that I worked there. Partying became a way of life and I loved it. Since drinking and driving was done all the time back then, that is exactly what I did. My life should have ended several more times, but miraculously, I would awaken just before my car hit a tree. I would hear my name being called, look up and get the car back on the road. I never equated my old friend's voice with God. How self-centered and egotistical I can be!

There was one man in my life that became the bane of my existence. He was a very large, ugly, evil man who delighted in the misery of others. He was lewd, crude and generally a disgusting human being but as a customer, I was forced to deal with him as best I could.

When I wouldn't date him, for obvious reasons, he tried to shame me in front of my friends and customers. My friends would tell me to ignore him, and most times, I did. But there was one time when I couldn't take it any more and I challenged him.

I was tending bar one afternoon and, as it was lunch hour I was very busy. I heard my name called but when I turned to ask what the customer wanted, I learned that he hadn't called me. I dismissed it and continued on with my duties.

The bar's owner had left for the day but the evil one remained. And, the torture began. The evil one was loudly announcing to one and all that I was a lesbian and that he had the pictures to prove it. Since it was a lie and there certainly were no pictures, I challenged him. I came out from behind the bar to go to the telephone to call the police. He began threatening me, telling me that he would break my back if I called the police. I was enraged and totally unafraid. I walked right up to him and, inches from his face, told him that he better kill me dead right then and there because I would surely kill him if I lived. I put my life on the line in front of fifty witnesses. He had no choice but to back down. He let his friends pull him out of the bar, threatening me all the way.

Once he was gone, my bravado left also. I ran into the ladies room to cry. Fortunately, one of the regular customers took over until I recovered. When I returned, people gave me their support and admiration. I sat down at the bar, thanked the customer for taking charge and ordered the first of several shots of Southern Comfort to calm my nerves. I was very shaken by the incident and it took an hour or so before I felt myself again.

It was later that afternoon when I remembered that just before the trouble began, I had heard my name called and realized that my shadow friend had sent me a warning. This was the first time that I realized that the voice was a warning. It certainly wasn't the last time I heard it, either.

I finally quit bartending and began to change the direction of my life. I moved to another town, worked at different jobs and generally found my life to be miserable. Life was the same struggle most single mothers endure. There was never enough money. I had an ancient yellow Toyota

Corolla that Lisa and I called "Myrtle the Turtle." Myrtle had no pep and hills were a trial for the old girl. I could handle that, but the fact that Myrtle was very old meant she broke down every time I turned around. Myrtle was putting me in the poor house but there was nothing I could do about it. I needed a car and didn't have the money to buy another one. I did the best I could.

I was lonely and looking for someone to take care of me. I felt as though I was a total failure. I had had enough of bill collectors calling, until my phone was shut off. And the electric company was threatening to do the same. I had defaulted on a loan and since I didn't have a telephone, the bankers came knocking on my door. Then, for the first time in my working life, I was fired from my job. I wasn't very good at it but I hated the fact that I was fired. And, finally a friend told me that I was a selfish user and a generally bad person.

As I was sitting at home nursing my wounds Madeline, my beloved godmother, died from breast cancer. Not having a phone I missed the wake and funeral. I was devastated that I didn't get to say goodbye to her.

I felt friendless, jobless, and penniless.

Among the few good things in my life that I could count on was my family, my daughter and my shadow friend. The one who lived in my heart was a part of me that I counted on.

I was dating a man and we had gone parking one night. We were kissing and I was getting heated up. I heard, "you're getting easy!" Well, I was so insulted that I pushed the man away, asking how he could say such a thing. Fortunately, he knew about my abilities and asked which ear I heard the comment in.

I indignantly replied, "my right ear."

He pointed out that if he had made such a comment, I would have heard it in my left ear. He made a good point. Needless to say, romance ended early that evening.

A few weeks later, as I was driving on a quiet back road to meet my boyfriend, I suddenly saw his car approaching. To my surprise, his former girlfriend was sitting in the car with him all snuggled up against him. They drove past me, not even looking my way. In surprise, I looked in my rear view mirror but the car wasn't there. I looked forward again, then back in the rearview mirror but I was still the only car on a road with no turnoffs. There could be only one explanation. I had had a vision of what was to come. I knew this wasn't a good sign and sure enough, when I arrived at our meeting place, he ended the relationship saying he was going back with his former girlfriend. I wasn't very surprised nor was I upset. Once again, my shadow friend had prepared me. If only he could make my every day life as easy to bear as this breakup.

It was the lowest point of my twenty-five years on this earth. I felt that I had failed in every way a person could. I was ready to give it all up and was trying to screw up the courage to commit suicide. My daughter, Lisa, was my savior at that point in my life. I had to live to take care of her but knew that, once again, changes had to be made.

PETER

I continued to party every other weekend. What else was there besides a dumpy apartment that had potential but that I could never afford to fix up, a beat up old car that was constantly breaking down, and an ex-husband who was not cooperating with me, nor financially supporting me and Lisa.

It was late spring when Peter came into my life and at the time he seemed to be the answer to my prayers. We met at the bar I had formerly worked at and talked for hours. We had unhappiness in common and he sympathized with my plight. We continued to see each other and he made me feel safe and understood.

Peter was of medium height and build with a halo of curly, light brown hair and eyes. He was average looking until you looked into his eyes. They are a normal brown color but the expressions and depth of feeling I saw in his eyes fascinated me. He was kind to me and Lisa, had a good job and his own home. He was "stable." To my eyes, red from crying, he was a knight in shining armor. It wasn't long before Lisa and I moved in to Peter's house. At first, things were rosy but three weeks after moving in, I knew that I had made a mistake. I stayed because I couldn't bear to go back to my miserable life and while I told myself that Lisa needed stability in her life, I realize now that it was I who needed stability. Lisa only needed to be loved and taken care of. And, I loved her so much; I was willing to do anything necessary to see that she had as normal a childhood as I could give her. What I didn't realize was how much Lisa disliked Peter. I thought her feelings were of jealousy. I truly believed Lisa resented the time and attention I spent on Peter rather than her. It seemed a natural reaction to a new situation plus the addition of another person. I was wrong.

Living with Peter, I didn't need to work outside the house but believe me, I worked hard. I kept the house clean, split wood for the fireplace, cooked, grew flowers and vegetables and was a model mother when Lisa came home from school. This was what I thought my life was supposed to be like, but I still felt as if something was missing.

Without my realizing it was happening, I was losing my friends and becoming estranged from my family. My mother disliked Peter intensely and I should have taken that as a clue! I knew that I was in real trouble when my grandfather died and I naturally expected to go to the funeral. Peter didn't agree and I couldn't understand why he had a problem with my attending the funeral. Standing at the kitchen sink, we fought over this and he slapped me across the face. I did the only thing I could I could think of to stop him from hitting me again. I saw a steak knife on the kitchen counter and grabbed it, wielding it before me. Yelling that bigger and meaner men than him had tried to browbeat me and failed, I defended myself. He saved us both by pinning me against the wall and agreeing that I would go to the funeral. I didn't go however, because I had a fat lip that I didn't want my family to see. Nor did I want to explain how it got there.

I went into the bedroom and sat on the side of the bed thinking of what had just happened. I couldn't believe that here was another man who thought I could be abused. What was it about me that made men feel they could get away with this? Could it be that I was so subservient because of my upbringing and only rage allowed me to express my true feelings? I knew that I had to make changes but was afraid to.

Life calmed down after that. Peter realized that I wasn't some weak willed woman who could be browbeat into doing everything he said simply because he said so. He may even have respected me because of it, but I couldn't say for sure. It wasn't an ideal life but one that I settled into and tried hard to be happy in. Lisa appeared to be doing well so I hung in there for her sake. I was making a compromise to be sure, and one that I would later regret.

As winter set in, I remember being very cold one day because I wasn't allowed to turn the heat on and I couldn't get the fireplace to stay lit. Peter had shown me how to do it, but I hadn't caught on to the trick of keeping the fire going. Peter wasn't too happy that he had to come from work to get the fire going. Eventually, I got the hang of it, though and life was going smoothly, as long as I kept my mouth shut and did as I was told. Shades of my childhood haunted me but I felt helpless to do anything about it. I guess I wasn't enraged, only sad.

Then, one morning I woke up and felt empty. Instinctively, I knew that my shadow friend was gone. I actually felt the loss and pain as soon as I opened my eyes. I immediately knew that I was different and that he was gone. I felt that, having compromised my life he was too ashamed to be with me any longer and left. The grief I felt was enormous and was with me for several years. I actually felt as if a hole had been cut into my heart. Even though I had Peter and Lisa with me, I felt lonely and knew that my life would never be the same. I continued on planting my gardens, splitting wood, cooking and cleaning.

I was psychically blind and lost. I was amazed at how much my every day life had involved psychic events.

I decided to get a job in order to get out of the house. I may like time alone but that only lasted for so long before I was craving companionship. This was the first step to leaving Peter but I couldn't admit it then, even to myself. I had lost my sense of self and needed to find out how to live my life without the psychic advantages I felt that I had. The job helped to re-instill a sense of myself. I became more confident, so much so, that, after three years of living together, I was able to leave Peter after a particularly bitter argument because I refused to be brutalized ever again. There had been enough of that in my life and I would not stand for it.

During the argument, Peter hit me hard enough to knock me down to the floor. In shock, no one moved for a few moments. Then I picked myself up, took Lisa by the hand and walked out of the house. Although I was determined to never go back, I had to get our clothes and other belongings. So, I did go back one time to retrieve our belongings and never went back again. Once again I felt that I had failed, that I had lost everything. I was homeless, furniture-less, and seemed to be unable to get out of my own way. When was I going to stop falling into the same painful pattern, I wondered? When was my life going to become the way I dreamed it would be? I told myself that it was over the next hill, that I had to keep moving forward and to stop making the same mistakes and following the same old patterns of failure.

CARLA

Not knowing where else to go, I found my boss, Roger, at the lounge he frequented. After telling him what had happened, he agreed that we could not go back. Roger knew someone who could help. He took Lisa and me to a friend, Carla, who was looking for a housemate. It was agreed by all that Peter was not to know where I was living. I was afraid of him at this point and needed to feel safe.

When we were introduced, I took an instant liking to Carla. A petit woman, 15 years older than me, she had a down-to-earth sense of humor that I could relate to. It was a sad time in her life though. Carla's husband was dying of cancer and she needed both financial and spiritual help. Carla and I took to each other like ducks to water. We felt that we were soul mates and were grateful that we had found a way to meet and be together. Carla had a fourteen year-old son living at home and a twenty year-old daughter who lived in her own apartment. So, Carla and I, with our children, began to create a happy home. At least as best we could as Carla's beloved husband lay dying in the hospital.

A few weeks after Lisa and I moved in, Carla's husband died. I accompanied her to the hospital to assist in making the appropriate arrangements and did my best to support and comfort her. I felt that having rescued me it was now my turn to rescue her.

As word of her husband's death spread the flowers began to arrive. Carla was taking pictures of the flowers and trying to decide which black dress to wear to the memorial service when the telephone rang. I had begun to screen Carla's calls for her so was surprised to hear Peter's voice on the phone. He had followed me home one night as I left work. I was horrified to think that he had been stalking me. My haven of safety was gone and I felt desolate. He had called to gloat at his success at finding me and I quickly hung up.

Later that evening, Carla decided to go out without me, as she wanted to be alone. I stayed home. My employers had a booth at a major trade event in Boston starting the next day. Being a small company, I was to attend, even though I was their secretary. Not knowing my way around Boston by car, my employers were picking me up early the next morning for the drive into the city. I was asleep when Carla came home.

The next morning, I saw that Carla's bedroom door was still closed. "Good," I thought, "She is finally getting some sleep." And, as quietly as we could, the kids and I left the house for the day. And, quite a day it was, too. At the close of the trade show day my employers began celebrating their day's success. Before we all got too carried away I called home to say good night to Lisa. Carla's son answered the telephone and told me that Carla's bedroom door was still closed and locked. A feeling of dread came over me and I said that I was on my way home. I looked at my bosses, explained what I knew and we all agreed that Carla was probably dead. But, that made it all the more horrid as the children were in the house with her.

My employers drove me home as quickly as possible. When we entered the house, I went directly to her room and tried to open the door but couldn't because it was, indeed, locked. We broke in but found we were too late. Carla had passed away. After calling the police, I called my sister to come take Lisa away because I knew it was going to become very scary at our house and I wanted to protect her from it.

The next few days were a living nightmare. The coroner had pronounced the cause of death to be suicide. I didn't believe it for a moment. Carla did not act as a person about to commit suicide and she adored her children—she simply was not ready to die. I have always believed her death to be accidental. She had been out, probably had a few drinks and still felt unable to sleep. So, I imagine she took tranquilizers or sleeping pills, never dreaming that she wouldn't wake up the next day. In my mind, Carla's death was accidental and that opinion will never change.

The double memorial service was difficult for everyone. As I sat listening to the minister talk about God's will as it related to Carla's death I felt so angry. It was obvious to me that this guy didn't know what he was talking about. What kind of God would let Carla and her husband die? What kind of God was leaving me bereft once again? It was during that memorial service that I became an atheist.

Carla's family had asked me to leave so I joined Lisa at my sister's. I had expected to be asked to leave but did not expect to have to leave immediately. I thought I would be given time to find a new place to live but I guess seeing me in her daughter's house was too difficult for Carla's mother. I was saddened by the entire experience and never blamed Carla's mother for banishing me. My sister agreed to allow Lisa and me to stay with her until I got back on my feet.

CHARLES

Lisa and I stayed at my sister's for two months. It was a difficult time for all of us. She lived in a small four-room apartment with her boyfriend. Four people in the apartment was two people too many. But, they never complained. After a while I came to realize that I had overstayed my welcome and knew it was time to leave my haven of safety.

In July, when I had saved enough money, Lisa and I moved into a new apartment in the same town where Lisa was born. We felt recovered from all that had happened to us and I was feeling strong enough to begin my life once again. I felt a great debt to my sister and [now] brother-in-law for helping Lisa and me get back on our feet. I no longer had any friends but hoped that I would make new ones. I was now twenty-eight years old and had nothing to show for it.

Shortly after moving in to the new apartment, Lisa and I got new neighbors. A married couple with their single roommate, Charles, moved into the apartment next door. Tall, blond, thin, and attractive, Charles was kind and had a gentle sense of humor. He was just what I needed. We began dating and I learned that Charles had many friends. As time passed, they became my friends, too.

Charles moved into my apartment, which was a great financial relief as well as being my lover. His mother had passed away many years before, so Lisa and I met Charles' father and stepmother on Thanksgiving Day. Here was something Charles and I had in common, he hated his stepmother as much as I hated my stepfather. I thought she was a lovely lady who treated his father with love and respect. That certainly didn't earn me any brownie points with Charles!

Unfortunately, one week later, his father was hospitalized with pneumonia and died. Charles went into a deep depression following his father's death, not that I could blame him. Charles developed a problem with alcohol, which was bad enough, but he was a nasty drunk. Things between us deteriorated and we split up with Charles moving out.

While apart, we both had brief affairs but still missed each other. We met one night to see if we could work our problems out and get back together. He promised to ease up on the alcohol while I promised to be more understanding and not badmouth him. We were happy and in love again. One week before my thirtieth birthday, we were married. Finally I felt safe and secure, and most of all loved. We had many friends and life was one big social whirl. After having no social life for several years, our busy lives became a soothing balm upon my spirit. I was completely relaxed and let down my guard.

Our life of partying went far towards my gaining weight. And, I did. I gained an enormous amount of weight. To be honest, I had been putting on the pounds before the wedding, but now I was fat. And, the fatter I got, the worse Charles' drinking became. I was unhappy with myself, but worse, Charles was disgusted with me. He told me that the only way he could bear making love to me was when he was too drunk to care what I looked like. His disgust was an open wound to me but no matter what I did, I wasn't losing weight. My belief that I was fat, ugly and completely unattractive remained with me during the entire marriage. Nothing Charles said or did to try to correct the damage he had done with his cutting words could ease the pain I felt. Our sex life became non-existent unless he was drunk and that was certainly no fun for either of us. His drinking became worse. Sex had become a gut wrenchingly horrible ordeal and finally I couldn't take it any more and left him.

Taking Lisa with me, we moved in with one of our friends, Rich, a teddy bear of a man. He lived in a house big enough for all of us to have our own room. Lisa and I were happy at Rich's because he was so much fun and there was no stress. I became relaxed and happy. I believe Lisa and I helped Rich as he was living alone in that beautiful, big old Victorian house. To this day, even though I have not spoken to Rich in years, I still consider him to be an old and very dear friend.

Charles called one night to talk to about our marriage. He told me that he would give up alcohol and attend marriage counseling if I would come home. He told me that he loved me and wanted us to try to put our marriage back together. Rich didn't believe that Charles would change but having already failed at one marriage I was willing to do whatever it took to try to save this one. Against Rich's advice, Lisa and I moved back home.

Charles and I went into counseling together and tried to put the pieces of our marriage back together. Family and friends were supportive and kind, which we very much needed. The counselor we saw was very helpful and allowed us to see what had become of our relationship and how to mend our wounds. We both felt betrayed by the other. I betrayed Charles by letting myself go and getting fat while he betrayed me by drinking and being cruel with his drunken words. Charles never believed me when I told him how much money was spent on his drinking. Another bargain made as part of our reunion was for Charles to take over the family budget. He was shocked to realize that I hadn't been exaggerating when I accused him of bringing us close to financial ruin by his drinking. It helped to keep Charles on the right path. He didn't touch a drop of alcohol for several years and our family life got back on track.

The marriage counselor we saw warned us that many emotional wounds had taken place in our marriage and that we shouldn't be surprised if we couldn't mend them all. Our sex life was one of those problems that were never resolved. Our counselor was also a hypnotist, and thanks to him I was able to lose 35 pounds. This didn't help our sex life though because I still believed that Charles thought I was disgusting. It didn't matter how often he tried to reassure me, he was never convincing. After three years of sobriety, Charles began drinking again.

Lisa had seen and heard enough to no longer want any part of Charles in her life. We formed an "anti-Charles" bond that was unfair to him but it kept my relationship with Lisa intact and was a piece of revenge for me.

I started a new job with a major corporation. I loved working there, had an enviable social life and to all outward appearances Charles and I appeared to be a happy well-adjusted couple.

One night in early June, Charles went on a rampage about the lack of sex in his life. He called me a frigid non-woman and that he had had enough. He wanted a 'real' woman in his life and told me that I had better get my act straightened out. I was shocked by the malice in his voice. Knowing that our neighbors had heard every word he said because all the windows were wide open and he was shouting, I retreated into the bedroom and cried all night. All I could think of was that I *did* want sex I just didn't want Charles to ever touch me again.

After six years of marriage, I decided it was time to end it. I had to acknowledge that while I cared about Charles and loved the social life we had, I was not in love with him. I felt that there was more to life that I was missing. I wanted to be completely and totally in love with a man who was totally in love with me. I knew that I could stay somewhat happily married to Charles as long as I didn't have to have sex with him, but felt that I was cheating us both if I stayed in the marriage for the sake of safety and security. I believed this was wrong; that I couldn't do it to either of us. I felt that Charles also deserved to have someone who was totally in love with him.

Telling Charles that I wanted a divorce was one of the most difficult things I ever had to do. I may have hurt people inadvertently but now I was going to intentionally hurt someone I cared for. I felt very guilty the night we finally spoke. In fact, so guilty that I went into counseling to help me deal with my guilt.

Charles was hurt, angry and I'm sure, felt betrayed. I was very sorry about that but knew in my heart that I had made the right decision. In time, Charles would find that woman who would love him, as he deserved to be loved. I believed that with my whole heart.

So, having made arrangements with Sue, a friend from work who had been looking for a roommate, Lisa and I moved out of the condo Charles and I owned. I'm sure that there are people out there who wonder why I moved out rather than Charles but the truth of the matter was that I could not afford to stay there and pay the bills by myself. Lisa was not Charles' daughter so he had no financial obligations to her and I certainly did not feel I deserved alimony. With Lisa's room now empty, Charles could get a roommate to help pay the mortgage.

It took time, but eventually Charles and I found that we could be friends. He has found someone that he is happy with and I wish him love and happiness throughout his life.

I discovered that I had learned a valuable lesson, one that I shared with my daughter, Lisa. When you have a difficult decision to make, look at yourself in the mirror. Having made your decision, can you look at yourself in the mirror and feel good about it? If you cannot, you must think about it a bit longer or decide that you are making a bad decision.

There were many financially difficult times after ending my marriage when I would look in the mirror to test if I had made the right decision. Life was difficult and I often thought of my safe, secure marriage where the bills got paid on time and I wasn't trying to decide whether to pay for the heat or buy food. I would look in the mirror and picture myself living that old safe and secure life again and would know in my heart that my original decision had been the correct one. As difficult as I felt my life to be, I knew that it had to continue as it was and let the chips fall where they may.

IT'S TIME TO GROW UP

After leaving Charles, I buried myself in my work and began moving up the ranks of the corporate world. I found that I excelled at what I was doing. My life began to change for the better and professionally I was ecstatic. I had started out as a temporary secretary and through four promotions in seven years I became a software product manager, then marketing specialist. It was a dream job that I loved every minute of. And they loved me right back.

When I was working as the junior software product manager, I was taken by surprise the day my manager called me into his office. As I made my way to his office, my brain frantically searched for whatever it was that I had done wrong. As I nervously sat down a manila envelop was pushed across the desk. With shaking hands I pulled out a letter addressed to me. I hadn't read very far before my chin dropped. The letter stated that I was being given 50 shares of company stock as a reward for outstanding performance! I knew that every year a recipient from our group was chosen to receive this prestigious award but it never occurred to me that I was even in the running.

I looked up at my manager with a puzzled look on my face. "What did I do to deserve this?" I wondered.

"You did a great job! You didn't have a clue what product management was about but you dug in your heels and learned all you could. You were the first product manager to accomplish a synchronous worldwide first ship date—even though you were told it couldn't be done. You pulled a large, professionally diverse group of people together and made them a team. And, you have earned the respect of everyone. What more can I say other than you can't tell anyone yet."

"The greatest moment of my professional career and I can't tell anyone?"

"I'm sorry but you must wait until it is announced in a few days."

After shaking hands, I headed back to my cubicle clutching that envelop. I felt overjoyed and humbled and wanted to shout my news to anyone who would listen but kept quiet.

When the announcement came, looking at the happy faces of my teammates was one of the proudest moments of my life.

Personally, life was becoming interesting. It's amazing what a divorce can do to friendships. While I knew that splitting our household belongings in half was expected, I was surprised and hurt by how many of our friends Charles got custody of.

A few of the friends that I had made through Charles remained my friends plus I had my best friend, Melanie, who remains one of my best friends to this day. These dear people were, and continue to be, my friends. And, as always, my family stood beside me once again. Even though, I imagine they were getting tired of helping me. They were as ready as I was to get my life in order.

My new roommate, Sue, was a social butterfly and together we made a formidable team when we went out. We always had a good time and the only stress I felt was the good stress of performing my job to the best of abilities.

My confidence was growing in leaps and bounds and then it happened. For the first time in many years, men were telling me that I was pretty. Who would have thought that anyone could think that I was anything but fat and ugly? After all, I still weighed twenty-five pounds more than I should. But to my surprise, apparently I was the only one who thought I was fat and ugly. Men were constantly paying me compliments and I began to believe that I didn't need a bag over my head, after all.

It was during this time that I began to study hypnotism, a subject that had always fascinated me. I began by reading stories of people who had been hypnotized and continued on to case studies of patients being regressed to past lives to aid in their phobia recovery. Again and again I read about angels being seen by regressed patients. I never made the connection between my old friend and angels. I was beginning to think that maybe there was a God, after all. I wasn't ready to transform from atheist to an agnostic, but the afterlife and reincarnation appeared to be real. I began to rethink my attitude towards God; that perhaps I had been looking at things through a narrow viewpoint. It was a small step but a positive one that went far in my return to God.

As the years went by, I continued to progress and grow at work, I had two intense relationships with men, made many friends and counted myself a success at life. I should have known better. Things began to fall apart. Again.

The major corporation that I, and many of my friends, worked at began downsizing for the first time in its history. While my friends and I were initially safe, we knew that the axe would find itself hanging over our heads soon enough. The man I had fallen in love with was laid off and the only place he could find another job was in a faraway state. So, with bitter tears flowing, we bid each other goodbye.

Lisa and I had moved into a different apartment only the two of us shared. We were happy there and our friends loved coming to visit. However, the cost of heating the apartment with oil kept me in a constant state of being broke. My telephone was cut off and I no longer had a car (it had been repossessed). Life was difficult once again. After one year my apartment's lease had run out and I could not afford to stay there any longer. My friends were as disappointed as I was because it was a great apartment and people loved being there. Meanwhile, I moved in with Jeanette, one of my friends from work.

Lisa had had enough moving about and decided to move in with friends, looking for the stability that I had never been able to provide her. She had grown into a beautiful young woman with green eyes and lovely, curly, dark brown hair. Like me, the blonde hair we shared as children got darker as we got older. My hair turned a dirty dishwater color while Lisa's became a beautiful dark brown color to match her father's. She remained slender while eating everything in sight. I warned her that she should slow down…that her weight would catch up to her appetite but it never did. Having been subservient so often in my life, I didn't want Lisa to turn out that way. I encouraged her to speak her mind and to never allow another person to use her as a doormat. God bless her, that's just the way she turned out. Occasionally, she didn't know when to keep her mouth shut so I put up with the angry phone calls from the orthodontist and the school system. I was determined that Lisa's life was to be better than mine. Lisa carried anger inside her that I didn't recognize and to this day, God help the male authority figures in Lisa's life. Maybe I should say, God help Lisa because jobs with a strong male authority figure don't last very long before she is seeking employment elsewhere. Most of the time, though, she is sweet, funny and well liked.

Life was going along well enough. I still had a job and living with Jeanette was nearly perfect. We were very compatible and happily lived together for a total of three years. Life at work was difficult because of all the lay-offs. It was hard saying goodbye to so many friends that I had made over the years. Jeanette was laid off and work in the area was non-existent. We were a good support team for each other. One of us was always helping the other in any way we could.

And then the axe fell on my group. Everyone was downsized with the exception of two engineers and myself. We were moved to a new group, given our instructions for finding and selling the software to a third party and prepare for our jobs to end.

While negotiating the sale of the software to a third party who had been a customer for the previous several years, I was encouraged to consider taking a job with them. The idea had appeal because even though it was far from home, my youngest brother lived in Chicago, only an hour away. After hearing the entire company, from the CEO and President to the engineers worked to convince me that I should come to work for them, my prospective manager (new to the company) began to interview me as he drove back to my hotel later that day. This man earned college degrees as a hobby so naturally his first question was "What school did you go to?" Never having been a successful liar, I admitted that while I had some college, the only degree that I owned was my high school diploma. Needless to say, the interview was brief and I was never contacted for that job again.

I went home devastated and slowly began to fall apart. Meanwhile, Lisa had turned 18 and was in love. Her boyfriend convinced her to move to Florida with him and they left. Lisa neglected to mention that she was leaving or that she was taking my car with her.

The cracker factory loomed large. I felt I had lost everything. The man I adored, the daughter I loved, and my dream job were gone. I was diagnosed with Panic Disorder and went into treatment. My days became a dull haze of tranquilizers and Prozac. I no longer recognized myself. Jeanette and I lived in a rural area far away from town and I began to fear being alone. I don't know why this happened but I felt that if I was left alone I was going to die of a heart attack because there was no one to save me. Philosophically I knew that I wasn't making any sense but I couldn't stop it.

I had taken a medical leave while waiting the three weeks for the Prozac to take effect. I had a lot of time to think about my life and didn't like what I saw. I spent many a neurotic hour reviewing all that had gone wrong in my life and finally came to the realization that there was a defect in my personality. I had spent my life trying to be perfect: a perfect wife and mother (let's face it—I wasn't), a perfect employee (I was very good but not perfect), my hair, clothes and makeup had to be perfect all the time (except for when I was sick or cleaning the house but God forbid I left the house without appearing perfect), and the shame I felt if anyone saw my home looking less than perfect (a rare occurrence but it did happen). And if every aspect of my life, if every minute of my day wasn't perfect then I would beat myself to the ground for being the worthless failure that I knew I really was.

Now, here I was a complete and utter failure in every aspect of my life, all at the same time. No wonder I was a basket case!

I was finally forced to admit to myself that I wasn't perfect and that I never would be. That was such a depressing thought, I cried for days. That's when my family and friends came to my rescue once again.

"Of course you aren't perfect! What a silly notion! No one is perfect and where do you get off thinking you are?" they asked. "If you were perfect, we wouldn't love you so much. If you were perfect, you wouldn't be the kind, caring person that you are."

"If I was perfect I would be kinder and more compassionate. I would be a better person," I cried. "I can think of many people who are kinder than I am."

"Get over yourself," they told me. "We just want the Linda we know and love to come back to us."

I cried for a few more days and when I stopped crying, I thought about what they said. And, slowly I came to realize that I was loved and accepted for who I was, warts and all. I was the only person who expected me to be perfect. I was the only one beating myself up for having those warts. It took some time for me to realize that I had been a real ass. And, that it was time I did something about it. It was time I learned to love and accept myself for who I was. Not an easy proposition but I always did love a challenge.

Eventually, I began to see myself as others saw me: not perfect but definitely a worthwhile human being. Once I accepted the fact that I was worthwhile, which meant that I was worthy of love and respect, I slowly began to accept my imperfections. I lost some weight and decided that size 14 was okay. I had to accept the fact that I would probably never be a size 6 but then again, I never was a size 6 so who did I think I was kidding? My daughter still loved me even though I hadn't been the perfect mother. My family still loved me despite the fact that I didn't live the life they wanted for me. I had to find a new job and I knew that anyone I worked for would be happy to have me as an employee. Men still found me attractive even if I carried an extra twenty pounds or so. (Okay, in my heart of hearts, I wish I were slimmer and to be completely honest, my body is my least favorite part of me. But, since I'm still "overweight" I guess it's really not a priority in my everyday life.)

As I gained my self-confidence back, I also began to reassess the people in my life. Having discovered who my friends really were, I began to take a second look at those who professed themselves to be a friend but really weren't. Slowly, those individuals were eliminated from my life. My theory was "who needs them?" My life is happier without them, and their negativity.

These were HUGE lessons for me to learn. And it was extraordinarily difficult to learn them but I'm glad that I did.

PART TWO

Gabriel

Ascended Master, Archangel
God's Messenger and Guardian Angel
My friend and protector

As a girl your presence soothed me
As a teen your presence enthralled me
And, as a young woman, I lost you

Now, in my middle years, finally, I met you again
Now, in my middle years, finally, I know your name
Now, in my middle years, finally, I know who you are

As always, you soothe away my fears
As always, you are my encouragement when I falter
As always, you walk by my side, keeping me safe from harm

My friend and protector

Linda M. Routhier

THE GOOD LIFE BEGINS

As my fortieth birthday approached I began to see a door in my mind's eye. I imagined that on the day that I turned 40 I would stand in that doorway and look back on the first 40 years of my life and say, "Thank God that's over with." Then I would step through that door and slam it shut! I looked forward to the rest of my life, which would be my reward. I was determined that the next 40 years would be filled with happiness.

My fortieth birthday came and went, and while intellectually I knew not to expect any "poof of magic," I was secretly disappointed that I hadn't magically transformed into the happy person I knew was bursting to come out.

The time had come when I had to make a decision on what to do with my life. My dream job had come to an end and I had to figure out what to do next. I had seen so many people laid off and now on Welfare because there were no jobs for us in the area of Massachusetts that we lived in. I was not going to put myself in the same situation so I decided that I had to move again. I wanted Jeanette to come with me but her family and friends were close by and she didn't want to leave them. I could understand that but I also couldn't stay. I knew that it was time to make changes in my life that had purpose and meaning. I didn't know what that purpose and meaning were but I was eager to find out.

One of my oldest and dearest friends, Bob, had an apartment in the basement of his house and agreed to let me rent it from him. So, I left central Massachusetts and moved to the "South Shore", a section of Massachusetts that is south of Boston but north of Cape Cod.

I was surrounded by friends and became happy and secure. After a couple of months, I felt safe enough to come off the Prozac. I still had a fear of being alone but I was no longer living in a secluded area and Bob was usually home. If he wasn't, there was any number of people who could be at my side within minutes. If a panic attack kicked in, together my friends and I would handle it. We were all prepared for the worse. I'm happy to report that only once did I need help with a panic attack. I am so blessed that these friends have been part of my life for so many years. After I was weaned from the medication, I became more alert. I had no idea how dull my personality had become. I felt as if I was being reborn.

I did occasionally have an anxiety attack but for the most part they were small and I could manage them. Fortunately, I never had to be medicated for Panic Disorder again. Anyone who has ever dealt with anxiety or panic attacks knows that part of the battle is telling yourself that just because things aren't going your way, you refuse to be a victim. Sometimes that didn't work and I would have an anxiety attack but they did become fewer and fewer as time passed. I haven't had a full-blown panic attack in six years now.

As the final days of my employment loomed, I took a real estate course and was now working as a real estate agent. I kept myself busy learning my new craft and making new friends. I worked up my courage one evening and called a man who had also been downsized from the same corporation that I was. For the first time in my life, I had a summer fling. While I was enjoying myself, professionally and socially, I got a call from one of my former real estate instructors, telling me that a new position was opening in our company. He had recommended me for the job and asked if I was interested in interviewing for it. Then, the Personnel Recruiter called to tell me about it and said that she had also recommended me for the job. Thrilled that they had considered me for the job, I agreed to the interview.

After interviewing with the CEO of the company and competing with six other individuals, I got the job. The CEO had a new subsidiary beginning and it was my job to make it a success. What a challenge! I couldn't resist and threw myself wholeheartedly into my new career. Shortly after, my summer romance fizzled away. I felt bad for a couple of weeks but someone was trying very hard to come into my life. I wasn't cooperating because I was hurt at how my romance had ended (but not at the fact that it did end) and this man was a recent widower. I saw failure written all over any potential relationship and was giving him a run for his money.

DAVID

David considers Bob to be one of his best friends and that is how we met. As David's wife lay in a coma, he would sometimes come by the house to visit Bob. Occasionally, I would be upstairs when David came over and slowly we became friendly. No one could miss how much pain David was in. His wife, Karen, was dying of cancer and David felt sad and helpless. Bob is such a fun guy and loved by all who know him. I'm sure that Bob was a balm David needed for his wounds.

I will never forget the day David came to tell Bob that Karen had died. Bob, Fran (another friend) and I were already there when David arrived unexpectedly. The three of us were sitting in the living room, while David stood and gave Bob the news. He described Karen's death in detail; how David had kissed Karen goodbye as she took her last breath. Bob, Fran and I were mesmerized by David's story. A short while later David left as he had many things to do to prepare for the wake and funeral. Upon David's departure, Bob, Fran and I just looked at each other in amazement. We could only imagine how difficult and painful David's experience was and we were amazed at his strength and compassion.

David continued to visit for the next few months and when my romance had ended, David began his pursuit. Naturally I was flattered that this tall, handsome, and charming silver-tongued devil was interested in me. But, he is ten years younger than I am and he drove a pickup, for Pete's sake. I did not date men who drove trucks. (Looking back now, I laugh at myself and call myself the snob that I was.)

My curiosity was piqued, however, so I asked my girlfriends about him. He had two reputations, one good and one bad. To his credit, David did everything he could to make Karen's last years easy for her and he never cheated on her. No matter how sick or how difficult her illness was for David, he stuck by his wife. This truly was a man who knows the meaning of "for better or worse." With my history, someone like David was like a beacon of light in the darkness.

Unfortunately, his bad side was very scary. They said, "He's a drinker." And, the Lord knows I didn't need another drinker in my life. But, David was persistent; finally, I agreed to go out on a date with him. Our first date was on my forty-first birthday. I was nervous because I had recognized that David was the type of man I could fall in love with. The date was a smashing success and I was giddy with delight. We went out to dinner and then dancing. I wore a silver lame dress that I had purchased for this special occasion. This type of dress was totally against character for me and I felt conspicuous wearing it. It certainly attracted attention! I felt uncomfortable having so many people looking at me. David had a way of making me forget that other people were around, however, and I had the time of my life.

We continued to date, each date more fun than the last. We started a habit that we haven't broken yet. Whenever we walk anywhere, we always hold hands. I imagine that we look sort of funny, as David is a foot taller than I am.

Lisa came home for the Christmas holiday and met David. I was very busy at work trying to get a large mailing out and in order to get it done early, David and Lisa came to help me. As they drove to my work location, Lisa gave David the third degree, wanting to know what his intentions with her mother were. David gave all the correct answers and we got Lisa's blessings.

In fact, Lisa went so far as to say, "It's about time you found a good one."

This made him ecstatic as he had declared his love for me and once again, I was holding back. As much as I wanted to be in love and as wonderful as David is, I was afraid.

The three of us were taking down the Christmas decorations, and standing by the wall unit, David told me that he loved me.

Without thinking, I replied, "I love you, too."

As soon as the words were out of my mouth, I went into a state of shock while David hugged me and Lisa shouted, "it's about time you admitted it" as she joined the hug. While they were celebrating, I was withdrawing, shocked that I had committed myself without thinking. For in my heart of hearts, I believed that I was David's transition girlfriend. I believed that he was on the rebound and that I was lucky enough to be his first girlfriend since Karen. Being realistic, I knew that someone as handsome and charming as David couldn't possibly want me. I was sure that after his wounds were healed we would part, he for women more suitable to his age and lifestyle. Other woman were calling him with invitations and he was sure to come to his senses and realize that he could be dating slender, young women instead of an overweight, over-aged me! David would tell me how beautiful I am but in my mind, I thought, "You're a young man and I'm an old lady, you'll get over it."

David persisted in courting me. I decided it was time for him to meet my family. It was a test and we both knew it, but I decided to go easy on him at first. We went to my sister's for dinner one evening and we all had a great time. My sister and brother-in-law gave David the thumbs up sign and welcomed him to the family. I was jubilant and ready for David to take the next test: my parents.

My family is as dysfunctional as many others so David met my mother, father, and stepfather all at one time. (How lucky for my siblings and me that our parents could put aside their differences for the sake of family unity.) My brothers and sisters were there to act as buffers, if necessary. It was. While my father and stepfather liked David well enough, my mother disliked him. David had tried too hard to impress my mother, the wine he wasn't used to drinking had gone to his head and he was at his silver-tongued best. My mother, who had had one wine too many, thought he was a jerk. I was very upset with both David and my mother. I felt she was being unfair but there was nothing I could do about it.

I was upset with David for getting tipsy while trying to impress my mother and ignored the fact that he was nervous. We had our first argument and I was thinking it might be a good time to bail out of this disaster before I got in any deeper. David wouldn't hear of it, of course, and promised to stop drinking. I agreed to trust him and have never looked back.

Then it was my turn to meet David's parents. I was very nervous and was happy to hear that they had given David their approval of me. His parents are so different from mine. They are still married and in love, for one thing. I was really impressed by that! They don't drink, go to church on Sunday, and still managed to have a happy life. This was a new experience for me and I felt good about meeting them.

When I met the whole family it was as if I was with my own. David's three brothers, and their families, were as much fun as I could hope for and the house was filled with jokes and laughter, not to mention good food. David's mother can cook up a storm for her large family and you can tell that she really enjoys it. She is like my sister that way. Both of them are always trying something new for the rest of us to taste test.

With the exception of my mother, both families liked our being together and I knew that my family was working to change my mother's opinion of David.

On June 1st, I moved into David's house and slowly, over time, made it my house. There were times, when I was cleaning, that I felt Karen's presence and would reassure her that I was taking good care of David and her home. As if she believed that I truly meant my words, I stopped feeling her presence. Only then could I begin to make our home mine.

In July we took a vacation and headed for Michigan to introduce David to my other sister and her family. As it is a two-day trip for us, we made plans to stay overnight at Niagara Falls. Standing with the colored lights behind us and the sounds of the Falls crashing into the water below David proposed marriage and I accepted. It was romantic and wonderful and didn't we surprise my sister when we got to her house. We all had a great time and after a week, David and I returned home.

Because of expensive repairs that needed to be made on our house, we postponed our wedding day for two years. I felt that, at last, I was completely in love and since this was to be my last marriage, I wanted to do it right. I wanted a wedding with a reception, immediately followed by a honeymoon. I had never had a honeymoon and this was my last chance. To me, it was worth the wait. Postponing my wedding for a new septic system was a joke that everyone at work enjoyed.

Work was becoming more interesting to me. The job was going well and I had been getting closer to my female co-workers. I had never worked with all women before and was nervous about it because I had heard that a group of women working together have a bad reputation. I'm happy to say that my new friends and I put that nasty rumor to bed. We got along so well, that as we became closer, there were no secrets and no subject was held sacred. We were brutally honest with each other and I began to feel blessed.

For a change, things were going my way. I was madly in love, had a nice home, a good job, plenty of friends and as always, my family. My mother came to know David better and thankfully changed her opinion of him. I was full of joy the day I heard her welcome him to the family and apologize for being wrong about him.

My forties were turning out to be what I had hoped for. The bad life was behind me and the good life was a long winding road in front of me. Or so I hoped.

MY NEW LIFE BEGINS

One of my co-workers, Sue, was recovering from colon cancer. The tumor was very deep which meant that the radiation treatments had affected several of her organs in order to reach the cancer. When Sue returned to work, she was still very ill and in much pain. There were times when I felt an overwhelming need to put my hands on her, thinking that if I did I could make her feel better. Then I thought to myself, "you're a loon and Sue will think you're crazy, too." So, I never followed through with my desire. Hindsight being twenty-twenty, I sorely regret not following my instincts. Because, when I finally confessed how I felt, Sue laughed and told me to feel free, any time I felt the need to place my hands on her I was welcome to it.

Sue's also a twelve-year breast cancer survivor. I was continuously amazed at her perseverance and belief in God. I couldn't understand how someone could go through so many treatments for cancer over the years and not be angry. Here was a woman who remained calm, kind and loving, always concerned that she was missing work and had an extreme loyalty to the company for allowing her to miss so much work due to chemo and radiation treatments. Her only complaint was the weight she gained due to the breast cancer medication she took daily to prevent the cancer from returning. Sue felt that her love of God, and his love of her, kept her sane.

In our growing friendship, Sue and I had several metaphysical conversations and realized that we were on the same wavelength. Except that Sue knew what she was talking about while I was bumbling along.

Knowing that there was more to life, reincarnation, God, angels, and other things, Sue unwittingly became my teacher. It was during this time when my atheism turned to agnostism.

Sue told me of a book, *Mary's Message to the World* by Annie Kirkwood, that she felt I should read. She told me that it was a wonderful book and would go far in convincing me that there was a God and rather than her trying to persuade me, Mother Mary would do a better job. I bought the book, read it and was impressed. Mary had such a soft gentle way about her when she spoke. My favorite part of the book was when Mother Mary told the story of her life with Joseph, including the birth of Jesus and His life. I never knew that Mary had several siblings or that she had children other than Jesus. I assumed that he was an only child. I imagine that those details were not important when His stories were written about in the bible. At least to me as I certainly do not consider myself an expert on the bible.

What I least liked about the book were Mother Mary's prophecies. She was much more specific than I felt comfortable with. Armageddon is not something I like to think about but I came to realize an important message that Mary was trying to make us understand: Armageddon does not need to happen. If people come back to God and live with Him in their hearts, all will be well. If we, as the human race, do not come back to God, the world as we know it will cease to exist. Remember those words, "the world, as we know it." This is a far cry from my belief that all life would cease and our planet would be blasted out of the sky. (And, I know that I'm not the only one who got the wrong impression!)

Sue and I had many conversations about Mary's messages. I was grateful that she had introduced me to such an intriguing book.

As I read more of *Mary's Message*, answers to questions I had had for many years began to be answered. I was beginning to believe that there is a God and was learning that he wasn't too happy with us as a human race. We aren't inviting God into our lives, we're not praying, and are generally living the life of pagans. Mother Mary repeated over and over again the need to pray and meditate and to make God a part of our daily lives. Slowly I began to pray. The Lord's Prayer, I'm ashamed to admit, was the only prayer I could remember, and I stumbled my way through it until, eventually, I could remember the entire prayer. I was embarrassed that I could not remember the Hail Mary and truth be told I still don't remember it. I learned, however that this was not important to Mother Mary or to God. She taught me that "real" prayers come from the heart and that conversations with God were preferable. What a concept! It took a while for me to be comfortable with these ideas however. So, to be on the safe side, every night when I went to bed I said the Lord's Prayer and then I talked to him. Making God a part of my every day life was yet to happen. For me, it was a long, slow process.

Meanwhile, Sue told me of an Intuitive Counselor in Florida, Laura Anne Walker, who had given an incredible reading to Sue's sister. I immediately wanted her telephone number as I was feeling the need for guidance. The combination of the upcoming wedding and exploring my budding spirituality made my head spin. I wanted to know without a doubt if, finally this time, I was going to get it right. I felt I needed help and that this woman could help me.

So, at the appointed time, Laura Anne gave me a reading that knocked my socks off. She reassured me that I was indeed marrying my soul mate and that I was about to begin a beautiful new life. Laura Anne described David as a "salt of the earth" type of man and, told me that I was opening up spiritually.

Laura Anne also introduced me to my guardian angel, Gabriel. I cried when I heard his name because she told me that he was my old shadow friend. Laura Anne explained that Gabriel had never left me. I was confused so she explained that I had, unintentionally, put up a spiritual block, or barrier, and now I must work to remove that block. I was upset to think that I had done something to keep my old friend from communicating with me. I couldn't understand how I had barred Gabriel from my life. I certainly didn't mean to. And, what did she mean that he was with me all these years and I was unaware? How was that possible? I had mourned the loss of my friend for years and now to learn that I hadn't lost him, after all, left me feeling relieved, happy and confused all at the same time.

Laura Anne explained that people have a tendency to feel ashamed of themselves. So ashamed, that we cannot face those who know us so well. Since we cannot hide from ourselves, we hide in the only other way we know. We protect ourselves by blocking out their existence. It is generally done with the sub-conscious, as I had done. But, it can be undone. It takes time, patience, prayer and a true desire to become whole again.

And, finally, Laura Anne told me that I had been a healer in many past lives and that I was a healer still. She advised me to begin meditating and to look for a metaphysical bookstore to aid in my journey. Since that reading, Laura Anne and I have spoken on the telephone several times and I now think of her as a friend.

So, feeling back in control and confident, David and I were married. Our wedding day was a wonderful one. We had planned for an outdoor wedding and clambake reception. For the previous several months I had prayed fervently for it to be a beautiful day. As the big day approached, I was very nervous because it had been raining for every day for the week prior to the wedding. My prayers were answered, however, as the day dawned bright and sunny. Most guests said it was the best wedding they had been to in years. And, my long awaited honeymoon was everything that I had hoped for.

SHUMALA

Several months later my wonderful new husband found a catalog for a metaphysical bookstore in our local newspaper. Flipping through it, he said that it sounded like exactly what I had been looking for and that it wasn't too far away. And, amazingly, they offered a course in their *'School of Energy Healing'*. The following weekend we traveled to Braintree and entered *Open Doors* for the first time. The sights and wonderful smell of this store entranced us. We spent an hour or so browsing and then left. Driving home, we agreed that I would be comfortable coming to *Open Doors* and that I should take the course. We discussed how we would pay for the six-month course, found a way and decided that I should go for it. The next week I went back and got an application. Again, I felt relaxed, comfortable and happy there. Little did I know that my life was about to change.

A week later, I was reading the story of gifted healer, Gene Egidio, in his book *"Whose Hands Are These?"* It was a Sunday morning and I had decided not to attend the meditation circle I had joined so that I could read this wonderful book. I was so moved by one of his stories of healing that I got on my knees, and with tears flowing, prayed to God to make me a healer. I had never sent such a fervent prayer to God but never had I wanted something so badly.

That afternoon, I returned to *Open Doors* with my completed application. While there I felt the need to hang around, so I browsed through the book and gift sections and finally decided that I was being silly. It was time to go home. I brought my purchases to the checkout counter and began

chatting with the cashier. When I handed in my application she introduced herself as Pat and informed me that she was one of the instructors
for the *School of Energy Healing*. While we spoke another woman
approached and joined our conversation. The three of us chatted happily
for a few moments and then it was time for me to leave. As I turned to walk
out the door, the stranger called out that it was nice to meet me. That
stopped me in my tracks, as we hadn't been introduced.

Normally, I would have just continued along but I turned around,
introduced myself and asked her name. She introduced herself as
Shumala. Well, that's a strange name and when I asked about it she told
me that Shumala is her professional name. You know, I just had to ask
and was told that she is an Intuitive Counselor and she was giving
psychic readings. Pat then announced that Shumala's appointment had
called to cancel. The two of them gave me a questioning look. Pat asked
if I would like to have a reading. Feeling as if I had entered the twilight
zone, I agreed. After buying a blank cassette to record the session, I
followed Shumala to a small room off to the left of the shop and sat
down across from her.

Shumala is a lovely woman with long dark hair; warm brown eyes
and an engaging smile. I immediately felt at ease and watched with
anticipation as she settled herself and placed the cassette into the tape
recorder. Shumala took my hands in hers and began to tell me about
myself. We spoke of many things that Sunday afternoon, including the
"truckload of Karma" that I came into this life with. But to me, the most
memorable part of the reading was being told that I was here on earth
to be a healer. All questions about what my purpose in life had been
completely dispelled. Shumala and I both felt that the day had been pre-
ordained. And, without a doubt, God had answered my morning
prayer. At the end of the reading we hugged goodbye and both felt
chills! I left the room feeling dazzled and overwhelmed. I immediately
left the store, got into my car and drove home. I made myself crazy
trying to make that recording of my visit with Shumala to work in my

car's tape player but to no avail. I couldn't get home fast enough to play it at home. To listen once again, to hear once again, that I was on the right path to being a healer. And, my budding spirituality was blossoming like a rose. I was beginning to feel that I was being guided onto a path I had never thought to travel. It was an exciting feeling. And now, with my feet firmly planted on the ground, I was ready to take the next step to becoming a healer.

THE SCHOOL FOR ENERGY HEALING

April 21, 1998 was my first night at the *School for Energy Healing*. I was nervous, unsure of what to expect. When I entered the area designated as the classroom, there were several people already seated and for the first few moments, looked as nervous as myself. Folding chairs were set in a semi-circle facing a white board hanging on the far wall. I took stock of my new classmates and began to relax. They seemed to be average people, just like myself. A few people were talking and I joined the conversation as we waited for our instructors. Other students had come in and now several conversations were going on. We were a noisy group when Richard and Pat, our instructors, entered the room. They later admitted how surprised they were by our comfort level as generally a new class is very quiet and waiting for someone to show them the way. It was a precursor to what an extraordinary experience the fourteen of us were going to have over the next six months.

We began our first night by introducing ourselves and explaining why we were taking this class. I related my Gene Egidio and Shumala story and couldn't get across what an amazing event that was in my life. Really a life changing experience not to be forgotten. Listening to the others introduce themselves I kept hearing the word "Reiki." I didn't have a clue what it was, but several people were practicing it and others were enjoying receiving it so I figured I would learn what it was at some point in the class.

Then we did the most extraordinary thing. We moved our chairs into a circle and Richard led us in a guided meditation. This was a first for me, as I had minimal experience with meditation, and I found it to be strange but also wonderful because it was a way for us to bond. Every class from then on began with the circle and all of us looked forward to it.

Our second class held another extraordinary event for me. After the circle and a short lecture, one by one each student had their "aura" photograph taken. As my classmates had their photo taken and rejoined us I was amazed at the colors surrounding each person. I couldn't wait for my turn and wondered if it would be a beautiful blue or red or orange. I was so disappointed when I saw it. It looked to be a combination of yellow and green, not even emerald green, which is one of my favorite colors but a funny green. As my classmates looked at it, someone asked who the baby was and if I was pregnant. As we all took a second look, sure enough there was a small figure over my head. One of my classmates asked if I was expecting a baby. We got chills when I announced that I wasn't pregnant but my daughter, Lisa, was and due to have her baby within the next few days.

You will have to understand that when I had my reading with Laura Anne the previous year, she told me that I would have a soul connection with one of my grandsons. My grandson, Devin, was born five days later. If this photo wasn't proof of a soul connection, I didn't know what was but decided to put it to the test. At the end of the next class, my aura was photographed again. Of course, the baby was no longer over my head because he had been born!

I didn't mention it earlier but that funny green color of my aura…the computer printout that accompanied that photograph stated that the colors (green, turquoise, aquamarine and blue) were those of a healer and a teacher. These beautiful colors didn't show over my head because Devin's soul was showing as yellow in the photo and yellow was not reflected in the computer printout. Another piece of the puzzle fell into place for me.

A majority of our time in class was spent in lecture, with Richard or Pat leading the way. I have to admit that sometimes I didn't get the subject matter at first. Too many new concepts were coming at me and I would have to think about our lectures for a while before things began to click.

I remember talking to Richard one night during a break. We were talking about prayer and I was embarrassed to learn that the question I was asking about was addressed in the previous week's lecture. While I remembered the lecture, I still didn't get it. So, Richard had to explain it to me again: when we pray for someone, we are sending healing energy to that person. How? Intention. When we pray for someone's good we are sending good intentions, which is healing energy. This was a concept that I needed to think about and absorb. To my mind this information was monumentally inspiring and I began to change the way I think of prayer and healing.

I lay in bed one night and begged God to forgive my sins of the past. I wanted so badly for him to accept me into His life. Just because I was Born Again years ago doesn't give me forgiveness for 25 years of sin. For the second time in my life, I wanted to be part of God and do his will.

And, the changes began. Once again, God had forgiven me. It seemed that He didn't care that I had denied His existence for so many years. All God cared about was that I was back in His life and that I had made Him part of mine.

Becoming a Healer

As the classes continued, we were introduced to several energy healing modalities: Therapeutic Touch, Johrei, Essene, Reiki, sound, crystals, dowsing, and Acupuncture.

On Tuesday nights, *Open Doors* offers free energy healing, with time volunteered by the various types of healers. Any donations given were distributed to the charity of the month. This is truly a wonderful gift that Richard gives to his community.

As class participants, we were expected to experience the various modalities. I'll never forget the night I ventured for my first energy healing experience. I had been instructed that I should have an intention in mind when I began. Being of sound health and living stress free, I chose to have the psychic block I put up years ago be removed. I wanted more than anything to feel my old friend, Gabriel, in my heart once again.

First I was to have a 15-minute session with the Dream Weaver, which is a sound healing device. Since it was a short session, I really didn't have any expectations for success but did want to fulfill my commitment. It was a pleasant experience and I promised myself that one day I would treat myself to a full one-hour session.

Next, I was delivered to Maureen, a Reiki practitioner. While Maureen explained the Reiki tradition of energy healing, I noticed that her hands had become very warm. We spoke throughout that session, as I was fascinated by what I was experiencing. I had told Maureen that my intention was to remove an energetic block and that I had already lay on the Dream Weaver. Maureen told me that the block was being removed. To her it felt as if small explosions were going off in my head. Really? I didn't feel anything! At the end of the 30-minute session, I felt great. So good in fact that after thanking Maureen I asked if there was anything I could do for her! In describing my Reiki experience, I would tell the curious that it felt as if a warm heating pad had moved along my body and that it was a delicious feeling.

Over the next few weeks, I did try the other energy healing modalities, but the Reiki session with Maureen was the one that had struck a chord in me. I wanted people to come away from my table feeling as good as I felt getting off Maureen's.

Finally, the day came when my classmates and I were to have our first healing sessions with real clients rather than practicing on each other. We were very excited. There were to be two apprentice healers to a client, except for one, as there were an uneven number of us that evening. I volunteered to fly solo as I wanted to put myself to the test. Did I have what it took to make someone feel better? Going it alone was the only way to be sure.

I had learned to channel energy through my hands via the school. As I had not been trained in any of the healing modalities, the session was to be what I call "straight energy healing". In other words, I lay my hand on another student and prayed that something would happen. There were never any guarantees.

My first client was a woman with back problems. We chatted for a few moments and I began. I decided to concentrate my efforts where her problem was and put my hands on her back.

"I'm ready when you are," I told God and immediately the energy poured through me in a powerful surge that was absolutely exhilarating. I excitedly asked my client if she felt it too.

"Yes," she said. "I can feel it in my back and it is shooting down my leg."

I kept my hands on her back for the full 30-minute session. When the healing time ended and I assisted her into a sitting position, I asked "How do you feel?"

She replied, "I feel wonderful. The pain in my back is gone and I have movement in my knee that I didn't have when I came here tonight." She demonstrated by bending her knee and swinging it back and forth.

I was thrilled! The last doubts of my healing ability and in God were dispelled in this one 30-minute session. As my mother used to say, "I was walking on Cloud 9 and feeling fine." My remaining clients for the evening each complimented my work, but nothing will ever compare to my first energy healing experience.

I must admit that while I was generally successful whenever I put my hands upon a client, I wasn't always the brightest bulb in class. I simply could not understand the concept of chakras (energy centers located throughout the body). I read about them, knew where they are located and what each chakra signified. That part was easy because it was all detailed in books. Putting my hands on someone and knowing if their chakras were open or closed was beyond my comprehension. I watched my classmates and instructors, listened to them and still I didn't get it. I was frustrated until one day while my eyes were closed and I was working with a client, colors began appearing in my inner vision. After watching my very own color show, I realized that the colors I was seeing were chakra colors. Slowly, I began to understand that if I placed my hand where the color designated, the energy surged through me into the client. Eureka! I was finally there! I no longer felt stupid and ashamed but felt as if I truly belonged. The pieces were falling into place and it felt great. Thanks to the colors leading my hands, I was able to feel the energy center of each chakra. And depending upon how much energy the client needed, I could tell if the chakra was open or closed. My healing skills took off!

The *School of Energy Healing* not only wanted to assist you in becoming a healer but also wanted to make sure that you would be a responsible healer. One way to facilitate this was to ensure you knew who you are as a person as well as a healer. In order to accomplish this, we had a weekend retreat entitled, "The Awakening."

All classmates and instructors were expected to attend and we were there in full force, plus additional people who had come for their own enlightenment. My classmates and I couldn't believe that others had volunteered to put themselves in a position none of us were looking forward to. Our mission for the weekend was to answer the question, "Who am I?" It seemed simple enough but it wasn't. We were each instructed to pair off and alternate every 10 minutes, telling our partner who we were. At the end of each 20-minute segment, we changed partners. It was an interesting experience as each of us delved deep within ourselves as we attempted to define who we were.

All went well until Sunday morning when Richard became my partner. To this day, I do not remember what he said to me; but at the end of his 10-minute discourse I lashed out at him with full fury. The poor guy backed up as I attacked him. He, of course, had to defend himself and somehow we lost time. It was very confusing, and upsetting, for us both. I had so much anger that had come out of nowhere and wouldn't leave. At the end of our pairing, it was our lunch break. Richard and I parted and went our separate ways, confused and angry, wondering what had just happened between us.

Later on that afternoon, we spoke about it and hugged to reassure each other that we still cared for each other. But I was changed and I didn't feel that I was changed for the better. Perhaps because I had all this anger built up inside of me that astounded me with its fury. I simply did not know why I had behaved so badly to Richard and I was embarrassed by the outburst.

At the next class, we spoke about it. Richard and I were amazed that no one had noticed our confrontation. I felt as if I had been screaming at the top of my lungs, but apparently I managed to keep it quiet. I was angry and anxious because I still didn't understand what had happened.

One of my classmates tried to provide me with an explanation for my outburst and while I knew she was wrong, I also knew that she was trying to help me so I decided to politely listen to what she had to say. While she was talking, a booming voice filled my head with the words "You are more than you are allowed to be at this time."

In astonishment, I looked around the circle of my classmates and instructors and saw that everyone was behaving normally and no one was looking at me. My friend was still speaking as if nothing had happened. When I repeated what I had just heard, that's when I got the funny looks. Looking back, I realized that the block I had raised many years before had begun to dissipate. The Dream Weaver and Reiki sessions were paying off.

The next morning, I called my friend Laura Anne Walker and told her everything that had thaken place in the past few days. I was very concerned about my continuing anger, what had happened between Richard and me plus the missing time we spent together, and finally, the message I received in my head. Could that message really have been from God? Laura Anne reassured me that I wasn't going crazy and that she thought she knew what was happening and that it was a good thing. I wasn't to worry and we scheduled an appointment.

At the appointed hour, Laura Anne began by telling me "You had an awakening."

"How appropriate," I thought, "since that was the title of the retreat."

"You threw a big switch and all your chakras blew open, especially six and seven. When this happened, your consciousness blended with the Divine. When this occurs for the first time, a person becomes very disoriented, can feel isolated, experience strange anger and emotional outbursts."

"What does that mean?" I wanted to know. This was scary and overwhelming!

"It is called a 'mystical madness,' she replied. "This always happens to first timers. The theory is that sub-consciously the ego is not ready to handle what is, and has, happened. First a person goes a little mad, then (s)he transcends and becomes very spiritual.

"Not many people get to experience this. Maybe out of every 1,000 who try, only one or two get it and you got it, without trying." This gave me goosebumps.

"The emotional outbursts usually happen before the transcendence; hence, your anger directed at Richard as if you were possessed was the precursor to the transcendence. It could have happened at any time, even if you were working in the yard. You were ready for it to happen. And the missing time spent with Richard was when you connected to the Divine. Since this happens to few individuals, you should be grateful, relaxed and happy. You are on a marvelous path!"

I asked Laura Anne, "Who is communicating with me when I hear the voice in my head? Is it my guardian angel, Gabriel?"

She replied, "It could be Gabriel, or your higher self. Some of what you hear could be God directly. This all comes with a price but one worth paying. You are forever changed and you may not go back to the way you were. Stay yourself. Don't let others try to mold you. You have been chosen. Stay exactly as you are. You will be helping more people that way."

At the end of the reading, I didn't know what to think or feel. I was awed, overwhelmed and embarrassed, happy and scared. Me? Chosen? What have I been chosen for? I didn't ask because I couldn't believe what I was hearing. I was also afraid of the answer.

I've been such a sinner most of my life. I've broken several of God's commandments, more than once. Why would God want me? Things like this only happened to "good" people. Not to people like me!

Could it possibly be that we are supposed to live the lives we do for a reason? Is it possible that I am worthy of being chosen for something beyond my comprehension?

God had forgiven me. Was this His way of showing me that I have been forgiven?

I felt as if I had too much to absorb. I needed time to think about this.

DISCOVERING REIKI

As if nothing had happened I went on with my life. I couldn't deal with the idea that I had been chosen by God for anything so I decided to ignore it...maybe it would go away.

My healing work at the school continued happily. I had mostly good days when I could channel the energy all night, but there were times when it felt as if nothing would happen. If I was tired or feeling stressed, I felt sorry for those volunteer clients who were stuck with me that night. I felt as if I had let everyone down, including myself. I decided it was time to do something about it. Since Reiki was the energy healing modality that I most responded to, I chose to become a Reiki practitioner. And through Reiki learned that whether I feel anything or not, the client does receive healing energy.

Reiki is the Japanese word for "Universal Life Force Energy", the energy of life itself. A practitioner learns that (s)he is an instrument of the universe. The universal energy, also known as Ch'i or Ki, is the essential life force of the Earth, planets, and stars. It is the same energy that surrounds all livings beings. In other words, the aura, or energy field, that surrounds all living things be they humans, plants or animals.

Once prepared, the practitioner channels energy via the hands for healing of the mental, physical, and spiritual planes. Reiki is applied to the head, face, torso, legs and feet while lying on your back and then repeated while lying on your stomach. All Reiki clients remain clothed, but shoes and glasses are removed. A client lies on a massage-like table, closes his or her eyes and is told to relax. It is not uncommon for a client to fall asleep during a session. The average session lasts approximately one hour. And, it is a truly wonderful experience. I've never heard of anyone not liking Reiki. Only those Reiki practitioners who have been "attuned" are able to practice Reiki. Reiki attunements enable the practitioner to become a channel for this universal healing energy. From the time of the attunement and throughout the rest of a practitioner's life, all that is needed is to place our hands upon ourselves or someone else and the energy flows automatically.

On August 14, 1998, the first half of my Reiki attunement began. There were five other students in my class. As the class began, our Reiki Master explained what we could expect for the next two days, as well as the changes within ourselves that we could expect for the next three weeks. During the actual Reiki attunements, we were told to expect anything to happen. We may burst into tears or laughter. We may have visions of any kind and then again, nothing may happen at all.

When it became my turn, I was instructed to sit on the folding chair with my eyes closed and my hands placed in a prayer position close to my chest. My first thought was that this would be a great time to meet my guides, but then decided not to so that I wouldn't miss a moment of what the Master was doing. Instead of allowing myself to be a part of the ceremony, I chose to pay close attention to the experience, as if from a clinical point of view. This was a mistake however, because my eyes were closed and I could only sense what was happening. It was a beautiful experience and when it was over, I returned to my place, sat down and tried to absorb what I had just experienced.

While I rested, my hands became hot and they felt tingly so I laid them, palm down, on my legs to absorb what energy was being channeled through me. Then I was bathed in a white light. I was in the light and channeling energy into myself and was thrilled!

When all students had received their initial attunements, the Master told each of us what she had seen during our individual attunement. With me she saw a "being of light, dressed in robes." I imagined it was a spiritual guide, or perhaps Gabriel himself. Someday I hope to find out who was with me at such an important event in my life. I decided that I would like to meet this being of light during the second half of the attunement. Meanwhile, I told my Reiki Master about being in the white light. She gave me a look of disdain that shouted "You in the white light? Don't be ridiculous." I began to doubt the experience that I had had. Perhaps she's right. Maybe I only imagined it.

Class number two began early the next morning. We were excited to learn that one of our classmates was a professional psychic. She gave me some information she had seen of me, which was a treat and a fun way to begin our class. One of the really interesting things she told me was "I see you in a white light except that it's not white but a very pale color."

Another classmate announced that she saw it as a pale silver color, and the psychic agreed. I told them about the white light that had come to me after the last night's attunement and we were all excited about that. They felt gratified for the validation that what they were seeing, was actually happening. I was happy that my experience in the white light had been validated and I was reassured.

During the second attunement ceremony, I didn't experience anything until the end. My eyes were dutifully closed, yet I began to see colors in my inner vision. First, indigo for my crown chakra, then a royal blue color shaped like an eye, obviously for my middle (psychic) eye. Then the attunement was over but I wanted it to continue so that I could see more colors! The Master had to signal me a second time that the attunement was over because I had ignored her first tap on the shoulder. Slowly I opened my eyes and returned to my chair. When the attunements were completed, my classmates and I spent the remaining class time practicing Reiki hand placements on one another.

That evening, as I lay in bed waiting to fall asleep, I decided to begin practicing Reiki on myself. When I placed my hands on my stomach and solar plexus, the white light came and my hands turned on! I was thrilled and amazed. It lasted for a few minutes but then I had a random thought and just like turning off a switch the light was gone and my hands turned off. I thought I had killed my new abilities so to be sure that I could still channel energy, I placed both hands on my stomach. Fortunately, I channeled as if nothing had happened. I hope that with practice, these moments in the white light won't be so fleeting.

The following evening, as I lay in bed preparing to fall asleep, I saw the color green, even though my eyes were closed! Since the heart chakra resonates to the color green I placed my hands on my chest. I began to immediately channel energy. I thought that since this was going so well perhaps I could bring the white light to me, but it didn't come.

The next day, as I sat in a meeting, the President of my company was reading a customer's letter that really blasted one of our competitors. I realized that no matter how often I blinked, the color orange was in the center of the letter. I thought back to my chakra colors and realized that orange is the color for the power chakra. I looked forward to seeing more colors.

Another aspect of receiving our Reiki attunements, my classmates and I were instructed, was to expect our dreams to become more vivid. I hoped so, as I rarely remember my dreams.

One week following my attunement, I woke up thinking that Mother Mary had been showing me a piece of her life, but unfortunately I cannot remember details of the dream. I hoped that my dreams would be more memorable after that.

I dreamed again.

It's market day in the village. It is a beautiful warm spring day. The sky is a brilliant blue with a few puffy white clouds. I knew that I was the young woman in the dream, even though she didn't look like me. I had the feeling that my dream was not located in America, but Ireland felt right.

I was shopping and saw a young man who appeared to be fond of me. While we spoke, we agreed to meet later that day. Apparently, the young man was my sweetheart. Later that afternoon, I was standing on the edge of a cliff looking out at the ocean. As I watched the incoming waves pound into the rocks below, I heard my name called and turned to face my sweetheart. Unfortunately, I was standing too close to the edge of the cliff. As I turned around, unknown to me my heels were too close to the edge. I fought to keep my balance but couldn't. Screaming, I fell to my death.

I woke up suddenly and looked around my bedroom to assure myself that I was okay. The dream was so real! What was this about? Did I have a past life memory? I knew it was possible to begin to have past life memories, but I didn't expect it to happen to me.

A few years ago, while hiking in the White Mountains of New Hampshire with two friends, we reached the top of the mountain we had climbed. When we reached the top, I was thrilled to observe the spectacular view spread out before me. Until I came too close to the edge of the cliff and looked down. I had such a horribly frightened feeling when I did that. I was truly scared! My friends, of course, thought this was funny and did all they could to keep my terror at a fever pitch. I was amazed at how terrified I was but now I see the reason why. However, I still have to remind myself that just because I died from the heights in one previous life does not mean that I will die if I get too close to the edge in this one. Just to be on the safe side however, I try not to push my luck.

One week later I had another dream. It was the first dream that I remember having since last week's past life memory.

My name was Xiang Ping. My parents and I were on a ship coming to America. I was not married but my parents were eager to change that. I think it was the early 1900's. I was mostly sweet and obedient but not very pretty. As an unmarried girl, I was not allowed out of the cabin, unless I was in the company of my parents. Once, while my parents were elsewhere on the ship, I sneaked out of our cabin to roam about on my own. I enjoyed being free and merrily set about exploring. Although I tried to make myself tiny so that I wouldn't be noticed, my parents caught me and were very angry. I was taken back to our cabin and beaten for being disobedient. For the rest of the voyage, if I wasn't with my parents, I was locked in our cabin so that I couldn't get into any more trouble and humiliate my parents. But, in my heart of hearts, I was thrilled with my small adventure. I was only sorry to have caused my parent's shame.

The dream ended there. When I woke up, I thought it was a pleasant dream and was grateful that I didn't die in this one.

Over the next few weeks I continued to have past life memories:

1. I was lying in bed, very ill. The room I'm laying in is dark but I can see the tops of ship's masts through an open window. The face of the man I loved is David (my husband today). He is sitting beside me looking down upon my prone frame, looking so sad. He worked as a shipbuilder, working on the USS Constitution. I had the feeling that David and I were to be married but I died from whatever illness I had contracted before the marriage could take place.

2. I had been traveling on a sailboat one bright sunny day. I was leaning over the side to look into the water when suddenly the boat keeled over and I fell over board. The water was choppy and I did not know how to swim. I was terribly frightened and yelling for help. My friend Marie (that is her name this life) saved me by throwing a life preserver and pulling me back into the boat.

Another fear explained. My father lives on a sailboat and my family has enjoyed sailing very much. I love the nice comfortable, smooth sail. But, if it is windy and choppy I am frightened. We have never been able to explain why but I don't like going fast, playing in the masts or keeling over and zipping along the way the rest of my family does. I see now the reason for my fright, which doesn't alleviate the fright I feel when I get on my father's boat.

Today when I see my friend Marie, I look at her with different eyes. First because our past life connection helped me to understand the immediate liking I felt for her when we met. And, secondly, I'm grateful that once upon a time, she saved my life.

I have known for a couple of years that David and I have many past lives together but I had always heard it from others. Now, I have my own memory to cherish. And I think how wonderful it is that David and I were a part of history. I'll never look at 'Old Ironsides' the same way again.

The Reiki attunement is definitely making changes in my life!

BECOMING A REIKI PRACTITIONER

Now that I was attuned, I was eager to begin working with clients, people who have discovered the benefits of Reiki and look forward to their treatments.

On Saturday morning I joined the healing circle at *Open Doors*. Every Saturday morning, many people come to the circle to meditate and pray for their loved ones, as well as for themselves. While there, I saw Maureen, the Reiki Master, who had given me my first Reiki healing. I sat next to her during the circle and as is always done, we all joined hands to begin the guided meditation. During this circle, I had a full color show happening behind my closed eyes. Then the white light came or I went to it, I'm not sure. At the end of the circle, I asked Maureen what the white light signified. She laughed and told me that when I was in the white light, I was connected with the Divine! While realizing that connecting with the Divine is a good thing, I still didn't understand what it meant. Since Maureen didn't seem to think connecting to the Divine was unusual, I didn't ask any questions.

While Maureen and I had our brief chat, I noticed that people stayed to talk in small groups, I moved off to the side and watched Maureen. There was something about her that I couldn't quite put my finger on but I felt a connection to her. Immediately, I could see that she was very popular and had a ready laugh. As I studied her features: average height and weight, curly, dark brown hair and eyes. I noticed that her eyes sparkled when she laughed and her entire face appeared lit from within as she talked to her friends. A few moments later Maureen left the group she was speaking with and headed for the exit. As she approached, I moved forward to intercept her.

"Do you have a moment?" I asked.

"Sure, what's up?" she replied

"I'm not sure if you remember me but I have a question for you."

Laughing, Maureen said, "I remember you. What can I do for you?"

Blushing, I told her, "I've recently received my first Reiki attunement and would like to begin volunteering my time on Tuesday nights but as an apprentice practitioner I need an experienced person to agree to work with me. For some reason that I don't understand I feel a connection to you and wondered if you would allow me to work with you on Tuesday nights."

"Of course. Did you want to start next Tuesday?"

"Oh, yes, if you don't mind. I would love it."

"Okay. I'll see you then." And, Maureen left to continue on with her day.

Thrilled, with a big grin on my face, I left too.

Tuesday night finally arrived and I began to discover the joy of actively practicing Reiki on a variety of clients. Being the rookie, I followed Maureen's lead as we worked on our four scheduled clients.

I was still a student in the *School of Energy Healing* so between class and volunteer work, I had many clients to work with. The difference now was that I was more in control energetically. I missed the whoosh of energy pouring through me, but I had gained control of the energy. It did not come and go with how tired or stressed I felt. It was now always there. A smooth stream of energy really is preferable.

Since Reiki works on the mental, physical, emotional, and spiritual planes, we worked with a variety of clients. Men, women and children came looking for ease from stress; pain relief; recovery from fears, phobias and traumas; and, looking for a way to feel their connection with the spiritual presence they feel. It was exciting to give aid to so many types of people with so different problems.

I enjoyed watching Maureen and the other practitioners in the room. At the end of a session, Maureen generally had a message for our client. Often it was something like "you need to laugh more" or "you need more joy in your life." Then, kindly, Maureen would ask me if I had received any messages to pass along to the client. More often than not, I didn't but occasionally I would get a feeling about someone and hoped that it was a correct message. I kept my fingers crossed a lot back then.

As a student, one of the most important lessons learned is that energy healing never replaces a physician's care; it does not matter which energy healing modality is used. Today, we are fortunate that mainstream physicians are taking note of the impact energy healing has on their patients. Clinical studies are being conducted proving that energy healing of any type increases the effectiveness of medications. Articles are being written about the impact spirituality has on recovering patients. You may one day see energy and/or spiritual healers by a physician's side when (s)he visits patients. At least I hope to see it in my lifetime.

We often had experiences with clients who come to us in pain but as we work with the client, we may feel that the pain is caused by an old, strong emotion. For example, one gentleman came to us with a persistent pain in his ankle. The ankle had been injured some eighteen years earlier playing hockey and it was still bothering him. I had the strongest feeling that the pain in his ankle was caused by an intense emotion that he was not aware of. I had read that anger, bitterness, and other such negative emotion seeks a weak spot in the body and reside there causing continued pain. When I concluded the session, I asked the gentleman if there were any old, unresolved issues that he could think of. I explained that if he had an old anger, the emotion could have sought out his weak ankle as a place to reside. He was surprised by my question and said that while my hands rested on his ankle, he had had the same thoughts and, that yes indeed, he did have an unresolved issue. He told me that while my hands were on his ankle, he had also been thinking that his old anger was the cause of his problem! That surprised, as well as, satisfied my need to know if my feeling was on the right track. Unfortunately, he did not return for further treatments so I do not know if he resolved his problems, either physically or emotionally.

One evening, at the *School of Energy Healing*, I was assigned to work with a client who had an issue with too much mercury in her blood. This problem was causing her many health problems that she wished to be rid of. Amazingly, no matter where I put my hands, she was pulling in so much energy that my hands felt as if they were on fire. She began to shake and shudder as if she had the chills with a high fever. When I asked if she was okay, she replied that it felt great, keep it up! I continued to channel energy and watch the gyrating on the table. I had a hard time believing that someone could react the way this woman did. I've never seen anything like it.

When we finished the half hour session, we went into the reading room while we waited for one of my fellow students to take over. As my client was sitting down and I was standing next to her, I placed one hand on her head, rationalizing that she obviously needed as much help as I could give her. The gyrating resumed as if I had never stopped working on her.

When my fellow student took over the session with this client, she continued to gyrate and then, after 20 minutes or so, calmed down saying she felt great! She had had a tremendous release of bad energy. She now felt so good she began hugging and thanking us. It was a great experience!

MICHAEL INTRODUCES HIMSELF AND JESUS COMES

Before I had my Reiki attunement, I had had a sinus migraine for four days when I finally decided that I needed relief from the constant pain. I had tried to practice Reiki on myself but didn't have the patience to keep my hands on my head. I called Pat, one of my instructors, and Reiki Master, and asked if she could help me. Thankfully, she had an opening for that day and I gratefully took it.

Pat used the same private room at *Open Doors* that Shumala had used to give me a wonderful reading several months before. As I lay on the table, Pat told me to call any of my own personal guides for assistance during the healing. I had read [in *Mary's Message to the World*] that if you ask, Jesus or the Brotherhood would come to be with you. I didn't know whom I should call, so I called everyone I knew or had heard about…Gabriel, the Brotherhood, and Jesus.

Following the one-hour session, I was still in pain but knew that it would be gone soon. Pat and I were chatting as we headed into the main part of the store. I casually mentioned having taken her advice by calling the Brotherhood and Jesus. She stopped short and said, "Wait a minute, did you say you called the Brotherhood?

"Yes," I replied.

"Well, the Brotherhood was here! I saw him." She was quite surprised and I was thrilled to think that my call for help was answered. I realize that at some point, I should stop being surprised and accept the fact that if Mother Mary, Jesus, Gabriel or whoever says they will do something, they will. Just because I cannot see them does not mean they are not there! Another lesson learned.

Several months later, now that I was working regularly with Maureen on Tuesday nights, I asked Maureen for a one hour Reiki session. I was feeling stressed as I had decided to leave the company I had worked at for four years. She agreed and we set up the appointment. Maureen explained that she had a private practice in her home and gave me the directions.

I arrived at Maureen's small white house and after we chatted for a while, she began to prepare for the session by washing her hands. As she was coming away from the sink, drying her hands, she looked at me and said, "I see you on TV doing a talk show, like Oprah."

There wasn't much I could think to say at that moment, so I delivered the ever so unsatisfactory, "Oh?" I mean, really, what could I say after a statement like that? It is too far out of the realm of possibilities for me.

We went into the small room set aside for treating Reiki clients. Looking around, I saw the massage table in the center of the room and a large bookcase full of books against the back wall. White lace curtained windows on opposite walls allowed plenty of light into her treatment room. On a small table, set to the left of a futon, I noticed a particularly vivid picture of Jesus. I commented that His eyes seemed to follow me as I moved through the room taking in the sights.

Maureen replied, "Yes, I love that picture. His eyes seem to shine, don't they?"

"Yes, they do. It's eerie."

"Okay, lie down and get comfortable," she told me.

I lay on the massage table and tried to relax. I was finding it difficult to calm my nerves, though I can't explain why I was nervous. Maureen sat down on the chair set at the head of the table. Placing her hands on my head, she began to immediately deliver messages to me. I discovered that Maureen could channel her guardian angel, the Archangel Michael, whom she called Spirit.

Surprised that she had the ability to channel, I said, "I didn't know you could do this. You've been holding out on me!"

Laughing, Maureen replied, "I haven't been holding out. I'm surprised, too. Normally a short message of encouragement is all I receive, but Spirit has a lot to say to you. I'm just repeating what I'm hearing."

"Do you hear it as if you and I are having a conversation? Do you hear it only in your right ear?" I wondered, thinking of how I heard Gabriel's voice when I was younger.

"No, not really, to both of your questions. It is hard to describe but it's as if having words in your head that don't belong to you. For instance, my thoughts are recognizably mine, they follow the thought patterns I use every day. But, when I'm receiving a message, it is almost as if the message is beside my thoughts. It is not so much hearing the sound of the words as knowing they are not my thoughts. As I said, hard to explain."

"And hard to understand, too," I commented dryly. "Here's something else I don't understand. If it is the Archangel Michael that is speaking why do you call him 'Spirit'? Why not Michael?"

Michael, through Maureen, replied, "I am speaking for all of the angels, teachers and guides surrounding you both."

"I have angels, teachers and guides here with me now?" I wanted to know.

Laughing, he replied, "Yes, child. You have many teachers and guides with you always. All humans do."

Filled with doubt, I looked around the room we were in. I didn't see anyone. I asked Maureen, "Do you see anyone?"

"Of course," she replied. "I see Michael standing to my right. The others are not showing themselves in detail but I can see their light."

"Light? What light?" I asked.

"It takes a great deal of energy for any of the spirits to make a physical appearance. It takes a tremendous amount for any of them to reveal themselves the way Michael is appearing right now," I was told.

"What does he look like," I wanted to know.

"He says to tell you that he is handsome," she said, laughing. "My favorite feature is his long blonde hair."

This was going to be very interesting! And, just think, the Archangel Michael! Maureen obviously had some highly placed friends. I lay quietly and waited to see what would happen next.

Spirit told me that I am a very old, high-level soul and that this will be my last time on this earth plane.

I didn't know what to say to that so I kept quiet and listened.

Spirit also told me that I am here in this life to be a healer. I enjoyed hearing that because here was someone in authority telling me that I am to be a healer.

Maureen had continued to give me the Reiki treatment and I was beginning to relax. I turned over onto my stomach and Maureen placed her hands on my back while I turned my head away from her, seeking a more comfortable position. All was quiet for a few moments and I was thinking about Michael.

And, then, suddenly, Maureen said, "Jesus is here."

I didn't say anything. Amazingly I didn't feel surprised but cried tears of joy that He had come. Maureen described Him as tall with long brown hair, dressed in robes, with eyes so bright there was nothing to compare them with.

He greeted me, "Child, I am glad to see you doing well."

"Thank you, Lord," I replied. I didn't know what else to say.

Through Maureen, Jesus said that he and I had lived many life times together as healers; that we knew each other very well.

"We do?"

"We have known each other since the days of the bible stories. You were one of the healers who followed Me as I traveled throughout the land spreading My Father's word."

"I did?"

"Yes, you and Maureen both. The two of you are old friends."

He also told me that I am one of his "special" children. I have been chosen. (Again, I'm told that I am chosen but still didn't understand what this meant, and still didn't ask. I was afraid of the answer.)

Christ said that I have many trials still to overcome, confirmed that David is my soul mate, and that it *was* my grandson Devin in the aura photograph.

I asked about Mother Mary's prophecies.

"You should not worry about Mary's prophecies as prophecy may be changed," I was told.

I replied, "It is not for myself that I am afraid but for the millions of people who will not know or understand what is happening that frightens me."

Christ instructed me, "You are only responsible for your own soul. Every soul evolves at a different pace. You cannot be held responsible for the souls of others."

He gave me this message to give to the world: "Love is everything. People must learn to love for only love will save the world."

I asked the Lord about my husband, David. I was looking for reassurance that we would always be together.

He replied, "Why do you worry about such a thing? Have I not told you that you are soul mates? As soul mates you cannot be separated for even when you are apart, you are together."

I felt greatly relieved. So, feeling bolder, I asked about the soul connection with my grandson, Devin. "Lord, I know that having a soul connection means that one of us is here to help the other learn needed lessons. Am I to teach Devin or is he here to teach me?"

"He is here to help you. I cannot explain further. You will have to wait to see the lessons Devin will teach you."

I lay quietly reflecting upon Christ's words. I have already discovered a new type of love. Thanks to Devin I have learned a grandparent's love for a grandchild, a very different type of love than I have ever experienced. I look forward to learning whatever lessons I must learn from Devin because I'm already thrilled with the lessons I have already been taught by him.

In the momentary silence Maureen told me that Christ was giving me healing energy, that she could actually see the energy stream from His hands into me!

"You are healed," was His message.

Maureen said, "Jesus is gone."

"Goodbye," I called out. "Thank you."

Maureen continued to give me Reiki in order to finish what she had begun. I didn't really understand why she carried on because let's face it, if the Lord Jesus Christ says you are healed, what more is there? Later on, I understood Maureen's need to complete what she had started.

In the few moments it took Maureen to finish, it felt as if the temperature in the room had dropped twenty degrees. We both felt cold and as I sat up, I started rubbing warmth into my arms. We both felt the temperature change and realized that we had been so warm in Christ's presence, that the room felt cold when he left. We excitedly talked about Christ's visit and Maureen commented that she should have known something was going to happen because Spirit usually doesn't have too much to say to her clients. But they had quite a lot to say to me.

Among other things, Maureen and I were told that we have been sisters in the past as well as friends. That would certainly explain the connection that I felt to her! It was later on that we learned that we shared the same birthday, that both of us have Madeline in our names, wear the same dress and shoe size, have the same tastes in food and the list continues to grow.

While still in the afterglow of our incredible experience, my class-mate Lisa showed up for her Reiki appointment with Maureen. We were very excited and took Lisa by storm. When I left Maureen's house that night, I was riding on Cloud 9 reviewing what had happened. Then I wondered how was I ever going to tell the world Christ's message? He plainly told me that I was to give the world His message but how was I to do it? I'm your average woman just trying to get through the days the best way I knew how. Not having an answer, I let it go to the same place being chosen went, to a dark corner of my mind where I didn't have to deal with it.

Two days later, at the end of class, I strongly felt the need to deliver the Lord's message with my classmates. Out of cowardice, I asked Lisa to stand up with me for moral support. We stood up, and because I was shaking so hard, we held hands while I told the class of Christ's visit. I knew that I was setting myself up for ridicule and expected to be laughed at. But I wasn't. As a matter of fact, when class ended several of my classmates approached and thanked me for sharing my experience with them. One classmate actually hugged me! At least half the class didn't think I was crazy, but I'm sure that a couple of people thought that I was going off the deep end. I was concerned about it until I remembered Christ telling me that every soul was in a different place and that not everyone would be prepared to hear what I have to say. I tell myself that a lot!

I was very uncomfortable sharing my experiences with family and friends. After the life I had led, I couldn't expect anyone who had known me for any length of time to believe it. Only half of me really believed it myself. We're average, every day people. Things like this only happen to people you see on television. So, the only people I ever told about this was my classmates and my husband—who, God bless him, didn't laugh at me and has been very supportive of me and my adventures.

MESSAGES

One month later, Maureen and I had another session together. As usual, Spirit was there. I asked if Gabriel, my guardian angel, was there. I was told that he was there along with my other spirit guides. I sent my greetings to Gabriel and thanked him for being there. I was informed that he is always with me that "all I have to do is think of him and he is with me." That's the way spirit guides work.

During the session, Jesus came again. He repeated His message, "We must love one another if the planet is to survive." He also told me that I am to be one of his messengers. (Now, I understand what I've been chosen for! It's frightening, though. I don't want to be thought a fool or a fanatic and be laughed at.)

I was also given a gift of love. I had the sensation of being cocooned in love. At the same time, Maureen told me, "The angels are wrapping you in a metaphysical robe of deep purple velvet with gold fringe. The robe is a symbol of the love being poured into you."

I cannot begin to express how marvelous it felt.

Jesus came to the fore again. He explained, "You must write a book."

"Me? Write a book? I'm just an ordinary person. Why would anyone want to hear what I have to say?" Feelings of being loved were quickly evaporating.

"Your story needs to be told."

"My story needs to be told? I don't understand. Why? Why would anyone care about my life?"

"Will you do it?" He asked.

What could I say? If the Lord Jesus Christ asks you to write a book, then you write that book! Shaking my head with misgivings, I agreed to tell my story.

When the session was over I wasn't feeling very confident. "You got me into this," I accused Maureen. "I don't work alone, you know. It may be my story but we're telling it together. Agreed?"

"Agreed."

Maureen and I had many sessions to better understand what was needed for this book and for our general knowledge. Jesus did not speak with me again for several months, though Maureen said that she could feel his presence in the background.

One of the questions I asked Spirit was what the book should be about. You see I had been dragging my feet about writing it. I found it difficult to believe that I was actually going to write one. Not to mention how difficult the subject matter would be. I do not make a habit of talking about my past and I'd be happy to keep it that way.

"Is the book really to be about my life? All of it?" I wanted to know.

"All of it," Spirit replied.

Another evening we spoke about angels and their jobs as relates to humans. Our guardian angel (and no matter what you think, you have one) is the spokes angel for the group of beings each of us has available to us. This angel is also the one who tries to keep us safe from danger.

Maureen told me, "Your angels are saying that you've kept them pretty busy in your past."

I replied, "At least they weren't bored." We all laughed about that. Imagine angels have a sense of humor!

I was told that when we have decisions to be made, the angels want us to come to them for guidance. Even if we cannot hear our angels, our intuition or gut feeling will often provide us with an answer. We must remember that our team of angels love us and are always looking out for our best interest and soul's highest good.

"Soul's highest good. What does that mean?" I wanted to know.

This is the answer I received, "Before humans are born, you make an agreement with your guardian angel to watch over and protect you in order to accomplish your soul's goals for this life's incarnation. Humans are never born without having a reason for being here, there are lessons you must learn for your soul to progress. If you do not accomplish your soul's mission, you will continue to reincarnate until you do."

In other words, if you think your life is miserable now, just think about having to do it all over again if you inadvertently prevent your soul from learning the lessons necessary for its heavenly progression. Personally, I shudder at the very thought.

If you have a troubling life, I can understand your reticence in believing that you actually arranged for all the bad things to happen to you. I certainly had trouble with that concept myself. But angels don't lie. We must accept it. And try to find the lessons our soul needs to learn. This isn't easy but worth it in the long run.

When we are born, we do not remember our previous lives and the lessons we have already learned. This makes it all the more difficult to accept that we actually agreed to be miserable. Or arranged for certain circumstances to turn our lives upside down. But, as I have worked to write this book and have been forced to relive my past, I slowly came to realize that I had to live my life the way I did so I could write this book. That was a very uncomfortable thought until I came to accept the fact that my soul had agreed to become one of God's messengers before I was born. To deliver the messages God and Jesus have chosen for me, I had to experience my life as I did. It's much easier to think of the people we know whose lives are just merrily going along, seemingly without a care in the world. They have their health and their mental faculties are in good working order. They are successful in their business endeavors and their children appear to be well behaved. What lessons do they need to learn? It is not for you and me to know but there are lessons for the happy, successful people to learn just as there are for those with difficulties. Count on it.

Now the time has come for you to think about what lessons your soul must learn in order to progress.

Think about it. And pray that you are learning your lessons. Ask your angels to assist you. They are waiting to hear from you.

REIKI PROGRESSION

I graduated from the *School of Energy Healing* in October 1998. It was a wonderful day. My classmates and I were excited and looked forward to the future. Several classmates were making plans to go on to the School's Level II class. When asked if I was going to continue on, before I could give an answer I heard the booming voice in my head again.

"Your journey follows a different path," it said.

I looked at my friends and said, "No, I'm following a different path now." Just don't ask me what that means, I thought, because I don't have a clue.

Fortunately, no one asked. They just wished me luck.

I had quit my job and was now working as a temporary secretary. Many people were surprised at my leaving and I was able to rationalize many reasons for leaving a management position to become a temporary secretary. But, the real reason was that I felt a need to be uncommitted. I could feel that major changes were coming and I needed to be able to move freely and focus my thoughts on those changes and for writing this book. Unencumbered from the challenges of maintaining a career, or the challenges of a new job, I would be open for the new journey I was yet to take. While it was sometimes a difficult decision to live with because it was a substantial cut in pay, my husband and I dealt with it. Thank God for David who never made me feel as if I had made a bad decision, even if I brought home less money. Who always says, "whatever it takes, baby, as long as we're together."

I decided to go for my Reiki II certification, thinking that I could bring in extra money by turning professional. I asked Maureen to be my Reiki Master, as we had now formed such a strong bond. The date was set, and I was very excited. I couldn't wait.

There are three levels with Reiki. When you are first attuned, or created as a healer, it is called First Degree. This is basically an apprenticeship. You are allowed to practice on yourself, family and friends. No money is exchanged. It is generally recommended that a Reiki I practitioner wait a period of one to three months before progressing to the next level. This is to give the new practitioner experience needed to understand the changes taking place. Often a new practitioner's health is improved. It is a very exciting time in an individual's life.

Second Degree Reiki significantly increases the amount of healing energy channeled by the practitioner. Also, a Reiki II is considered a "professional" and may set up an office or healing area within the home to practice. It is recommended that a Reiki II practice for six months to one year before progressing. The reason is, once again, for the practitioner to gain skill in working with so many different types of personalities and ailments. Reiki III is the Master/Teacher's degree. This allows the Master to attune others as Reiki practitioners.

The big day finally arrived. At the appointed hour, I arrived at Maureen's house ready for the new experiences I felt sure were to follow. After all, look at all I had experienced after my first Reiki attunement.

After the lecture and practice, it was time for the attunement. I did not have any new experiences but Maureen commented that the room was full of angels, that I had drawn a big crowd. I couldn't imagine why. As I moved through the room, I asked if I was getting in any angel's way.

"No," she laughed, "they move fast." (That was a strange feeling!)

I did notice an increased ability with my healing work. I was also more confident as to the work I was doing. I felt that my healing experiences were more intense, as well. Regular Tuesday night clients seemed to notice a difference. I did not, however, become a professional. I really didn't feel that I had the time to do healing on a regular basis. I continue to do volunteer work and referred out clients looking for healing on a regular basis. This is more comfortable for me. The time will come when I will make Reiki a full-time career—but that time is not for a while yet. I can wait.

GABRIEL

Maureen and I continued to work together to learn as much as we could about this book. We agreed to meet weekly, whenever possible, to do research. I purchased a tape recorder just so that I didn't have to rely on my memory when Maureen channeled but it didn't work no matter what we tried. After a few non-recorded sessions, I gave up. I may be slow sometimes but I do catch on after a while. What really bothered me was that the tape recorder worked just fine when I brought it home. Obviously, these sessions were not meant to be recorded.

As a rule, we did not have Reiki sessions, but rather I sat in a chair or lay on the couch. Maureen put her hands on my head and immediately begin to channel. While she channeled I would chat with Spirit.

Some conversations we had were:

David was scheduled to work in Maine for 4-6 weeks. I was terrified of being alone while he was away. I was afraid the Panic Disorder would come back. I asked Spirit about David's leaving.

Spirit said, "David needs to go away to do his work. It is good for him. You also need this time alone for spiritual growth and to do the things you wouldn't do if David were around. You have no reason to fear, you are never alone. Just look over your right shoulder and know that we are there with you."

I asked if I would ever be interested in gardening again. The response was, "Yes."

I asked Maureen, "Is Gabriel *the* Gabriel, as in the Archangel Gabriel?"

"Yes, of course he is. What did you think?" she wanted to know.

"Well, I don't know. Why would I assume that he's the archangel? He could be an angel named Gabriel. How would I know? There must be more than one angel named Gabriel. I just thought I'd ask," I defended myself.

Remembering an event of many years past, I related the story of a presence, within a glowing light, that appeared during a bible study and wished to know who had come.

"Gabriel appeared that night," Spirit replied.

"He did? Why?" As wonderful as it felt to know that Gabriel had come, I was confused.

"He says, 'There was going to be a crisis in your life. Gabriel came to cushion the blow, to give you the support you needed,' Spirit said, through Maureen.

Maureen asked, "Do you remember what happened to you a few weeks after this event?"

I thought about it for a few moments then answered truthfully, "No. It was almost thirty years ago. Whatever happened wasn't spectacular enough to remain in my memory bank. All I remember is being more gifted, having more intense physic abilities."

"Well, your consciousness was changing and Gabriel was there to make sure that the changes didn't happen too quickly. If the changes you were to experience happened at a pace faster than you could mentally handle, you risked damage to your nervous system. This was a good thing that happened to you," Maureen told me, "It was, indeed, time for the shift in your consciousness. Gabriel was protecting you."

"Thank you," I sent to Gabriel as I looked in the direction I hoped he was standing at.

Maureen laughed and said, "He says you are welcome."

Another evening, Maureen and I were talking before the session. I asked, "How will I know if an idea belongs to me or if it had been planted by an angel?

Maureen replied, "To see if your idea belongs to you or to your angel, put it into the white light three times. If it stays in the white light each time then you will know that it is an angelic message. If it does not stay in the light, it is yours." (Easier said than done is what I say.)

When we began our session, immediately Maureen said, "The angels liked that analogy. It is a truism."

In another session, Spirit asked me "What do you want?"

I replied, "I want it all. I want to do everything, go everywhere, experience it all."

"Done," was the response.

I liked that answer so we continued. Not to burst my bubble but I was reminded that I still had trials to overcome. I realize this and feel that the first trials will begin if this book gets published. I'm worried that people will not look at me quite in the same way and that is frightening. I must remember what Jesus told me, "All souls evolve at a different pace. You cannot be responsible for any soul but your own." It doesn't necessarily make me feel better, though. Even now when people hear that I am writing a book of my spiritual journey, the conversation immediately ends. No further questions or comments are made, or some laughed as if to say, "You? On a spiritual journey? Yeah, right!" It is very strange.

One night, as I closed my eyes in preparation for the session to begin, I saw a cinnamon colored disc. Suddenly the disc had a black center, then the black was gone and the disc was once again solid. After describing my vision, I asked Maureen, "What's this all about?"

Spirit replied that, "It is a gateway."

"Gateway to what?" I wanted to know.

"The gateway between our worlds. You have a visitor. Your Grammy is here."

"Grammy Green (my father's mother) or Grammy O'Leary (my father's grandmother)?" I asked.

The exasperated reply: "Grammy! Just plain Grammy!"

"Then it must be Grammy Green because I never called her anything but Grammy but my great-grandmother was called Grammy O'Leary. Hi, Grammy, what are you doing here?"

"I occasionally pop in to see how you are doing," she replied. "I must go now but I will be checking in on you again." And, she was gone. I saw the cinnamon disc open and close at the same time that she left and I knew that she really had left. This was so exciting. When I went home that night and looked at my grandmother's picture, it was with a feeling of love renewed and it was a moment to treasure.

During another conversation I asked Gabriel if angels ever come to people as they do in the show, Touched by an Angel. I was told, "Yes, angels do appear as humans."

I asked for an example and before I knew it, I began to think of my dog, Blackie, the one our family had when I was twelve. Blackie was a big dog, half Boxer and half Black Labrador Retriever and very protective of us kids. The rule of the house was that if one of us were going somewhere other than the park next door Blackie was to be kept in the house until we were out of sight because we lived on a very busy street and he could get hurt trying to follow us.

On the particular day of my memory, I had just received my allowance and gone to the corner store to spend some of it. I must have been inside the store when my sister looked out the kitchen window to see if it was safe to let Blackie out. When I came out of the store and stood on the corner talking to friends, Blackie saw me and darted across the street. He was struck by a hit-and-run driver and dragged forty feet before he somehow got loose. As the car drove past me, with my screaming dog being dragged behind, I went a little crazy with hysterics. My memory ended there.

I asked Gabriel what part he had played, as I didn't remember anyone in particular being there.

He replied, "I was a bystander, standing behind you. I was there to protect you. I held you from behind to keep you from going to Blackie. You were fighting and kicking me and screaming hysterically."

"You kept me from going to my hurt dog? Why? Why would you do that to me?" I demanded.

"To protect you. It would have been too traumatic a sight for you to see Blackie up close. To block your view I kept you behind most of the crowd that had gathered."

"Had traffic come to a stop on both sides of the road?" I asked.

"Yes, there were many adults there to take care of your dog. Then the police came and gently lifted him onto a blanket as your mother arrived on the scene."

"How did my mother know what had happened?" I asked.

"I sent people to tell her and you pointed to where you lived," he replied.

Fortunately, Blackie survived that terrible day and my entire family took turns caring for him during his recovery.

Shaken, I changed the subject. I asked if there had been other occasions where Gabriel had come to my rescue.

He replied, "I have come at other times in your life but nothing extraordinary, nothing that would stand out in your memory because you were not in tune so you didn't notice anything."

He began speaking of the traumas I had suffered as a child. Gabriel explained that the blackouts I endured during my teen years were used to give me healing as there was no other way to give me the type of healing that I needed.

"What are you talking about?" I wanted to know.

"You were suffering from trauma that you could not mentally handle. We needed a dramatic way to give you the healing you needed. You not only needed healing from us but you needed people to notice that you needed help. So, we would take you out of body to give you a quick healing and to those people aware that you were just standing there not responding to them was a very dramatic way to bring your condition to their attention."

"It didn't work, though, did it? The abuse continued and the black-outs continued," I thought. I mentioned to Maureen that I also fainted a lot back then.

"It was an escape for you," Gabriel said. "You sometimes needed a way out of a situation that frightened you so you fainted."

"Well, I don't remember fainting on purpose, but it did work. I would be left alone for a while after a fainting spell."

This was too much for me to absorb at one sitting. I needed time to think as I was feeling overwhelmed. I ended the session.

Much was explained to me that night. As happy as I am to know that angels are among us, I do not like looking back on my past. It can be too disturbing now that I have such a happy life. But I must remember that I wouldn't be who I am today if I hadn't lived my life the way I did. I must remember that life is a series of lessons to be learned. And I'm so very grateful to Gabriel and the other angels and guides who have watched out for me all these years. Makes me wonder what I would be like today if there were no angels watching over me, protecting me. I probably would have died years ago. Or maybe I would have become a madwoman.

What do you think your life would be like without angels protecting you? Do you see many changes in your life that you could thank your team of angels for?

PROMISES KEPT

David left for his job in Maine. I was very frightened to be left home alone. Ever since being diagnosed with Panic Disorder, I've had difficulty being alone at night. The very idea of it made me run to my doctor's for a mild tranquilizer prescription. A protective measure, to be sure.

With bottle of tranquilizers in hand, one Sunday afternoon, I tearfully kissed my husband goodbye. The night loomed large in my mind. I kept telling myself that I was not alone. I had Gabriel and my other angels with me. They had told me that I was never alone and I did believe them. Up to a point. If I couldn't hear or see them, how much comfort could they bring?

Silly me. David was gone for a total of five weeks. In that time I saw him three times. And, I never took a tranquilizer. I never opened the bottle! The angels truly were there with me and for me.

That first night I was nervous about going to bed alone. I had determined that I was not going to take a sleep aid. I wanted to put my angels to the test, as well as myself. They didn't let me down. As I lay on my bed, knowing that I was psyching myself out and trying not to, I heard "Gabriel" in a quiet soft voice. And, I knew I wasn't alone, just as I was promised. I fell asleep.

The next night, as I getting ready to fall asleep, I heard the most beautiful sound I've ever heard. The angels were singing! They were singing me to sleep. But I no longer wanted to go to sleep. I wanted to hear the angels. Before I knew it, it was morning and I realized that I had slept like a baby.

Whenever I remember the sound of the angels singing, I can hear it again. I hope that someday they will sing for me again.

While David was away I was given the gift of many wonderful experiences. You can read about them in the next three chapters. I learned many new things but best of all, I learned that I am truly never alone and that I am always being protected.

Think about putting yourself in my place. Don't worry you are already there and never alone. And always loved.

MOM

I had decided that since David was away that it was a good time to take a week long vacation. The plan was to be on retreat while staying at home. There would be minimal interruptions as the weather was warm and the dogs could stay outside during the day while I rested, meditated and wrote. My quiet time was shattered with the news that my mother was in the hospital and had been diagnosed with emphysema.

Suddenly her death was not so very far away and I didn't know what to do about it. I knew that I should get to the hospital in New Hampshire and begin taking care of her but I didn't do anything to help her. I felt frozen, paralyzed with fear. I'm ashamed to admit that I was not dealing with the horrible news very well, at all. I wanted to bury my head in the sand and forget all about it. I would help others deal with stress and pain.

That night, Maureen and I were doing our volunteer Reiki work. Pat, one of our regular clients who had been diagnosed with terminal lung cancer came in. Lisa, another Reiki practitioner, was also drawn to work on Pat. Maureen told us that three of Pat's angels were there, celebrating because Pat would soon be returning to them.

I looked at Pat and said, "You know why they're excited, don't you? They need a fourth player for cards and you're it!" We laughed and Maureen continued.

The angels told Maureen and Lisa that Pat was special…she's one of God's messengers. They also said that Pat belonged to them and not to us. At that point, Maureen told us that Jesus was standing at her feet, with open arms, as if he was waiting for Pat.

But, while Lisa and Maureen were getting messages, I watched Pat's breathing become easier and slower. Her face and body became very still and long periods of time were passing between each breath. I thought, "Oh my God, she's dying."

While I was anxiously watching her, Pat took a deep breath and smiled. Then she whispered that she had gone away to a very nice place with flowers. She said that the flowers symbolized Maureen, Lisa and me but didn't know if we were flowers or if she was supposed to buy us flowers. Speaking for myself, I said we were flowers because I didn't want Pat to feel she had to go buy us flowers. (If you knew Pat, you would know that she would go right out and buy us flowers!) Maureen and Lisa echoed my words. I knew that Pat had gone away and was very grateful that she came back.

After Pat left *Open Doors*, the others came to see if I was okay. I was very shaken by what I had witnessed and felt that we would not see Pat again. That perhaps she would not make it through the night. Maureen agreed that we may not see Pat again but felt Pat would live longer than I expected. Fortunately, much to Pat's doctor's surprise, Maureen was right.

I was thrown into a state of confusion that I couldn't understand. At some point, I realized that the expression on Pat's face was that of a woman I had been quite fond of in my past, whose death I discovered. Unfortunately for me, Pat resembled my old friend Carla, and the similarity was painful for me to see. I was starting to get angry.

The next morning I was still mad and kept remembering the events of the last night. In my mind, I was yelling at God, Jesus and the Angels, saying that they couldn't have her yet, she still belonged to us. I was pacing my house, quite distraught, knowing that what I was doing and saying didn't make any sense but I was very upset. I forced myself to sit on the living room couch and asked myself why was I behaving so badly. It just didn't make any sense. Suddenly, I realized that I was angry about my mother and was transferring those feelings to Pat's situation. Once I recognized what was happening, I started to calm down and decided to write about it.

While I sat at my computer desk, typing away, the telephone rang. It was my mother. She was calling to say she was home from the hospital and needed me to come, as she needed my help. While admitting to mom that I wasn't handling her illness very well, I thought that God sure knows how to make you face your fears. We hung up and I cried for a short time, pulled myself together, and left for my mother's place in New Hampshire.

I arrived three hours later and found myself to be at peace with her illness. It was a long drive and I had a lot of time to think. Having come to my senses, I spent a lot of my travel time praying and thanking God for just about everything I could think of. I'm so glad that I did because when I saw my mom, with the oxygen tubes in her nose and trailing behind her, I was able to handle it. This unit that my mother was now attached to didn't look too scary but more like a humidifier with a long clear plastic tube coming from it. Later on, I saw the 5-foot tall oxygen tank in her bedroom.

On the way to my mother's place I had stopped to do her grocery shopping. After putting the groceries away, we had lunch and played cards for a couple of hours. My mom was very tired after that and laid her head down on the table. I began to give her Reiki, as my hands had been hot to get to her for quite a while. She asked me to stop however, and having no choice, I did. I was comfortable with saying goodbye as she wanted time alone to get used to her new circumstances. I decided that it was a good time to insert humor into the situation and as my mother crossed the room, I started to sing, "Me and My Shadow." Mom, not to be outdone, changed the words to "Me and My Snake." We giggled and that's when I knew that we would be all right. I kissed my mother goodbye and left.

By the time I returned home that evening I felt at peace and ready to handle what comes next.

As long as I remember that God doesn't give us more to handle than we can bear.

MADELINE AND GABRIEL

I received a gift. I was at Maureen's house, feeling stressed and was prepared for her to make me feel great again.

Often when beginning a Reiki session, the client's energy field is scanned to see how they are doing. Mine was approximately one foot above my body. This is generally considered good; but, while I'm in fine shape energetically, emotionally I was in need of help. As soon as Maureen sat down and put her hands on me, she commented, "oh yeah, there's lots going on here!"

The first thing to come through was this book. Maureen was channeling and told me that David was going to be prominent later on (I hadn't yet written about my husband). At some point during the session, I asked what I could do to help David to recognize the fact that he has his own angels to thank, instead of him telling me to thank mine. The response was that David would become enlightened, but in his own time and that I'm not to worry about him. Also, I must meditate more and ask for guidance. Once I do this, the ideas will come flowing through in abundance.

Maureen told me that there were several angels all around the room. Different angels were making comments and we were joking and laughing with them. After yesterday's crisis with Pat and my mother, I had some humble pie to eat, which I did.

I asked Maureen, "Do they know I am sorry about my bad attitude yesterday?"

"Oh, yeah, they know."

They did but had some comments to make in return. One angel said that I should be sorry, that I was bad. Maureen was laughing when she relayed this to me.

I was laughing, too and said, "Come on, I'm giving you a run for your money."

Another angel commented that I surely kept them busy.

I replied, "It's better to keep you hopping than to live a boring existence where you never had to do anything!"

They agreed.

After a few moments of silence, I asked if the angels knew what had happened to my beloved godmother Madeline. "Is she an angel or has she reincarnated?" I wanted to know.

"She's a Guide and is here tonight!" Maureen told me.

"She is? Where?" I asked.

"Standing next to you on your left side," Maureen replied.

Maureen asked if Madeline could give me some indication so that I would know that it was truly she.

Madeline told me, "I am your encouragement. Do you ever feel it when I tap on your shoulder?"

I never have but will be looking for it now. Maureen, who can see the angels and guides, asked me what Madeline had looked like when she was alive.

I described her, "Tall and thin, beautiful, a former model, with dark hair worn in a pageboy."

Maureen asked, "Is Madeline funny?"

I replied, "Not only was she funny but any party that Madeline attended was a success because she told great jokes and stories, played the guitar and sang and I had loved her with my whole heart."

Madeline said, "I always wanted to be a clown."

Suddenly Maureen saw Madeline wearing a clown's red nose and a Bozo wig. We had some chuckles over that.

Madeline told me, "It is so beautiful where we are; there are many flower gardens. You will love it when you got here."

I do love flowers and gardens and enjoy the small one I have at home.

Madeline said, "I am always here for you. All you have to do is ask for my help and you will have it."

She also told me that she would come to me in my dreams. (I can only hope to remember the dreams the next morning!) After what seemed but a short moment in time, Madeline said that she had to leave and did.

Following Madeline's departure, I felt warm with love and totally happy. I lay quietly, with my eyes closed, for a while basking in the feeling. A few minutes later I began to think of Gabriel.

"Is Gabriel here?" I asked.

Maureen replied, "He has stepped forward. There's also a group of angels here for you, at all times. And just as Michael is the spokes angel for my group, Gabriel is the spokes angel for yours."

Thinking of Maureen's words, I knew that Gabriel is the angel who watched over me as a child and who kept me alive so many times in my turbulent past. But, not realizing that there was a group of them I was surprised by her comment.

Maureen told me "Gabriel is an Ascended Master, which is a very high level angel who is in direct contact with the Divine."

I asked, "Does that mean that I connect with Gabriel when I connect with the Divine?"

"Yes." I was told.

I asked, "Will the time come when I, too, will be able to see and hear the angels?"

"Yes. You have the gift of communication."

Maureen told me that whenever I meditated and asked for Gabriel, he would always be there. She also said that I was welcome to ask all Ascended Masters to be there for they would come, and were in fact there now.

I replied that the meditating candle I always burned was called 'Ascended Masters and Guides'. I loved the scent and had been attracted to that candle from the first. She looked at me and said that since I was calling them (even if I didn't realize that I actually was), that they were there and ready to help however they were needed. This certainly puts a new spin on my meditating!

Since Gabriel has been such a major force in my life, I was curious to know what he looked like.

Gabriel said, "I'm handsome, of course."

I laughed and said, "Of course."

Then Maureen described him in detail. "Gabriel has waist length, dark, wavy, hair. He has a devastating smile, but doesn't show his teeth and his eyes are lit from within. He is wearing a gorgeous burgundy velvet cape over Three Musketeer-type clothing. He is wearing a doublet, hose and boots. He also wears one of those large, plumed hats. Gabriel is tall and is, indeed, handsome."

I asked, "Is his outfit from the French Revolution?"

She replied, "His clothes resemble that time period but I keep hearing that Gabriel is a knight."

I thought, "Weren't the Three Musketeers knights?" but kept quiet. After all, who was I to argue?

Instead I asked, "Have Gabriel and I had any past life connections?"

Maureen was given a vision showing that, in very primitive times, Gabriel and I were brother and sister. We held a very close bond to each other. She saw us huddled together, promising to always take care of each other. And, since that time we always have. Now as it is my turn to be in this plane, Gabriel watches over me. When Gabriel takes human form, I watch over him. It has always been so and always will be. I cannot describe the feeling I had at this time, other than to say overwhelming happiness.

Maureen said, "You and Gabriel are like two peas in a pod."

I extended my right hand out and swore that I felt a weight as if someone was holding my hand. I asked Maureen about it but she said that she couldn't see anyone. I have to admit that it could have been wishful thinking on my part.

As I mulled this over, and all was quiet, Maureen said that Christ had come. I was very pleased. I had missed him and prior to the beginning of the session had hoped that he would come. In my mind's eye, I dropped into a deep curtsey. He said something that I missed in the excitement of his return. Maureen commented that she was feeling pressure from behind and that her hands had become very hot. Then Christ said, "Love and Light," and was gone. It was a very brief visit compared to some visits we have had in the past but after such a long absence it was a joy to know that he still cared about me and took what time he could spare to tell me that he loved me. I remembered the first time Christ came to us. When He arrived, I wasn't surprised but cried with joy that He was there.

While I was lying there, absorbing this visit with Jesus, Maureen said, "Angels-In-Waiting."

"What?"

Maureen said, "The room is lined with chairs on all four sides and angels are sitting there…waiting."

"Waiting for what?" Was the logical question but she didn't have the answer.

"Does everyone have angels-in-waiting?" I asked.

"Yes."

"If everyone on the planet has a group of angels-in-waiting," I commented, "how many angels there must be!"

"Endless," was the response.

Suddenly I was in the white light. At the exact moment I realized that I was connected to it, Maureen said, "Welcome to the Divine."

I put my hands on hers and said, "I'm there." I was surprised that she knew I was connected. I was so amazed by the experience that I almost lost my connection but steadied myself and remained.

The angels-in-waiting asked, "How can we help you?"

Surprised because I had never known what happened when I was connected to the Divine, I didn't have a ready answer. All I knew was that I was in a white light for a time and then I wasn't.

"I-I-I don't know what to say," I stammered. "I wasn't expecting to ask for anything." I thought about it and then asked for help with my mother.

"Done," was the reply.

I asked for help quitting smoking and was told, "The instant you decide to quit, you will." (Rats, I thought. Free will is not to be taken lightly!)

Lastly, I asked if someone would extend my thanks to Lisa and Devin's angels because they are doing a good job and I am grateful.

A smiling angel replied, "We will be happy to deliver the message."

I was also told, "Ask for our help in making decisions. It doesn't matter if the decisions are big or small, just ask." Then the light was gone and all was still.

Maureen took her hands from my head and said, "When you connected with the Divine, a jolt of energy went through my hands and you were connected." She also commented upon how much she liked Madeline and how she loved the clown get up. Then Maureen began to measure my energy field again. This time she had to stand on her tiptoes and stretch as high as she could. She was really struggling to get the full height.

Jokingly, I suggested she get a step stool. Finally Maureen was able to stretch high enough to feel the top of my energy field and said that she had never felt one as large before. The field easily extended three to four feet above my body. I have never seen one as immense either. Out of curiosity, Maureen took her pendulum and began to measure my chakras. Each one, in turn, immediately began to spin in wide circles. The longer the pendulum stayed on a chakra, the larger the circle became. It was really something to see and we were definitely getting a big kick out of it. I was wide open and receptive!

When Maureen was finished, I slowly sat up. I didn't have anything to say for a while. There was too much to absorb.

I have been given a gift tonight, one that I hope to never forget. So, now it is written and will become part of this book. For all you non-believers of angels out there, believe. No matter how difficult it may be for you to accept, believe that this can happen to you, too. And, remember, God, Jesus Christ, and your own personal teams of angels love you and want the best for you. Never forget it.

I can only hope that you will begin to realize how lucky you are.

QUESTIONS

The next morning, I meditated before I began my day. And, as promised, I felt that Gabriel, the Ascended Masters and others were there to be with me. So many small details, forgotten last night as I wrote the previous chapter, came to me as I meditated. I decided to get my pad of paper and pen. I began writing as additional details were remembered.

I remembered Spirit telling me to meditate with pen and paper and the ideas would flow through. This morning they did, just as he said. I also noticed another major change: Maureen was no longer channeling Spirit, who had been the go between for me and Gabriel. Maureen was now channeling Gabriel plus several additional angels on my team. This had only happened once before when my paternal grandmother popped in for a quick visit. I'm sure Spirit was in attendance but I know his voice when he channels through Maureen, and I did not hear him at all last night. Obviously, Maureen continues to grow and strengthen at the same time as I do.

I connected with the Divine this morning just by thinking I would like to. I could not see angels-in-waiting, but I now knew they were there and imagined myself addressing them. I thanked the angels for being there; told them I loved them, and then I removed myself from the white light. After having spontaneously connected with the Divine for several months I now had an understanding of what was happening. Previously, I simply reveled in being in the white light but it didn't really have any meaning for me. Others seemed to understand what "connecting with the Divine" meant but I was clueless. Now, when I make the connection, I understand what is happening and can adjust to being connected.

A thought occurred to me. If this was happening to me, it had to be happening to others around the world. What a wonderful gift people are receiving. We are so fortunate to be able to hear, see, and feel how much we are loved. When I walk through my house and comment on how blessed I am, after last night that statement takes on a whole new meaning.

Other questions came to me. Since Gabriel is an Ascended Master and we are two peas in a pod, does this mean that I am an Ascended Master as well? What type of clothes do I wear when I am in spirit form? Does my costume match Gabriel's or do I prefer a different type of clothing?

So many questions waiting to be answered. I ended the meditation and began my day.

NEW EXPERIENCES

On Saturday morning, Pat had an appointment for a private Reiki session with Maureen. I asked if I could assist in the healing and got the nod to join in. When Pat arrived for her appointment, it was hugs and kisses all around. I was grateful that Pat was as happy as I was for me to be there.

The session began with Pat lying on the massage table, Maureen at her head and myself on Pat's left side. I immediately began to see blue, green and yellow chakra colors so I allowed the colors to guide my hands. While Maureen covered Pat's entire body, I stayed at Pat's mid section. When Maureen was working on Pat's feet, she whispered to me that there was a huge, white angel standing behind her and was leaning over to place his hands over Maureen's.

"Really?" I whispered back. "Who is it?"

"I don't know," was the reply.

Later, after Pat had turned over to lie on her stomach, Maureen told us that there was a host of angels standing close together surrounding the table and that each angel had both hands placed on Pat's body. It was an unbelievable sight for Maureen to see! Pat's body was covered in angelic hands and Maureen was informed that a major healing was taking place.

During this same time, the color white was now in my vision and at first I thought that I was connecting to the Divine but remembered that the colors I was seeing were Pat's colors. Perhaps Pat was connecting with the Divine. After a few minutes, I saw a wide band of orange come diagonally across my vision. This was unusual enough but then I realized that there were rips in the orange band. I have no idea what this signified and if any of you, dear readers, know, please tell me. I also saw two black circles surrounded by blue. In my mind, the black circles represented Pat's cancer-filled lungs and Maureen thought the blue represented healing.

When the session ended, Pat was not coughing and gasping for air, symptoms that had ceased shortly after the session began. As Pat sat up, the three of us were talking about the amazing events we had experienced during the one-hour session.

Pat told me, "It's interesting to hear you talk about colors. You've been on my mind all week and whenever I thought of you, I saw a rainbow."

I smiled because if I was to represent something, a rainbow is beautiful and I felt privileged to not only be on this wonderful woman's mind but also to be symbolized in such a beautiful way.

While we spoke, I had closed my eyes for a moment and saw the color fuchsia for the first time. Maureen told me that fuchsia is her favorite color. When Maureen said that, 'light dawned on marble head' when I realized that the color I predominantly saw is royal blue, one of my favorite colors. I closed my eyes again and this time I saw a golden window, arched at the top, in a black background.

"Whoa! What's this all about?" I wondered, but no answer came to mind. Much later that afternoon, as Maureen and I parted company, we were amazed that five hours had passed. It felt as if only a short time had gone by.

The following morning, Sunday, I woke up feeling exhausted. I let my two dogs out at 6:00am and then went back to bed until 8:00, something I rarely do. When I first woke up, but hadn't yet opened my eyes, I realized that I was seeing a color show! That never happens. After a couple of moments, I opened my eyes and got out of bed. I puttered around the house for a couple of hours and decided that I had better meditate before I changed my mind.

I started the CD player, lit my candle, made myself comfortable and closed my eyes. After a couple of minutes, the color show began telling me that I was in the proper meditative state. I always enjoy seeing the colors and today was no exception. I began to notice shapes in the colors that had never happened before. I got frustrated because every time I focused on the shape, it would be gone. For the first time, the colors were rotating in a counter-clockwise fashion that reminded me of the movement of the chakras. Twice, however, the colors spun so fast I got dizzy. I opened my eyes to stop the motion. Finally, the blues were in a white background but looked liked a drop of water that splattered rather than the smooth round disc I usually saw. I didn't understand what's happening but am sure that this will all mean something at some point.

Then, in the time it takes to blink, I very clearly saw an old black station wagon driving down the street, with a white dog hanging out of the passenger window. Then it was gone and I felt a shifting in my stomach and I was seeing colors again.

Before I had a chance to understand what had just happened, I encountered an old woman walking down the street. She had such a surprised look on her face! It was as if I had just appeared out of nowhere. Then, feeling the shift again, I was back in the colors. If what I saw was real, I hope that she was okay. Is it possible that I really did appear in front of her and that my sudden appearance was the cause of her slack-jawed expression?

These thoughts had no sooner passed through my head when suddenly, I was flying and looked down upon a white dog with large black spots. It wasn't a Dalmatian but I couldn't determine the breed. It was standing on grass beside a doghouse.

Back in the colors, then flying and watching waves come on shore.

I don't know what to make of today's experience but it was a lively one. As the day passed, I began to realize that I had been going out of body during the meditation. I was determined to be more in control the next time I meditated. If I was going out of body, I wanted to know that I was going and that I would be able to return. I have to admit that the experiences were fun and exciting!

Unfortunately, that didn't happen. The next night, when I meditated, I worked to recreate the exact same circumstances of my previous experience. I lit my candle, played the same CD, sat in the same chair and closed my eyes. It did take quite a few minutes to quiet my mind, and eventually I was in the colors but as I entered, there was a definite shifting feeling in my stomach. This happened several times. I did not go out of body that I know of. At the end of the session, I felt that today's lesson was to teach me to discern the shifting feeling that I feel both when I go out of body as well as when I return.

It is my belief that the previous night's session with Maureen was the beginning of my training. Maureen and I discussed this on the telephone and she agreed that I am being made ready for something. The experiences definitely have the sensation of being lessons. I have a feeling that life is going to get even more interesting in the future.

When I closed my eyes to go to sleep last night, I was in a lavender light. I opened my eyes and the light was still there so I closed them again, thinking "how pretty." Slowly the light faded, and I lay there wondering, "What was that all about?"

The next evening, as Maureen and I left *Open Doors* when our healing work was finished, I asked her about the lavender light and was told that it was a healing light.

"God sent me a healing light?" I asked. "Really? Why?"

"Well, He must think you needed it," she laughed.

I walked away in awe.

QUESTIONS ANSWERED

David returned from Maine at the beginning of May. I was so happy to have him home. I made a huge 'Welcome Home' banner that stretched across the front of the house. I wanted everyone to know that he was home again. As exciting as my life had gotten while he was away, I was happy for it to return to normal. Except for the dogs and my cat. Even though David was home and sleeping in our bed, the dogs and cat continue to sleep on the floor next to my side of the bed. They had gotten into the habit of protecting me and weren't ready to relax their guard.

A few weeks later, I had arranged for another Reiki session with Maureen. I was in a new job and the chair I was sitting in was uncomfortable enough to make my upper back feel strained. And, really, to be honest, it's a great excuse to communicate with my angel team and Gabriel. I've become an "angel groupie."

After catching up on each other's news, we got down to business. I lay down on the massage table and closed my eyes. Almost immediately, Maureen said, "Christ is here. He is standing off to your bottom left, near the window."

Although my eyes were closed, looking in His direction I exclaimed, "I can see a bright light in the left side of my vision." This was the first time I could see this much of Jesus. I was thrilled! "Welcome, Lord. Thank you for coming." I'm always happy to see Jesus.

He said, "I am always with you but I do not always show myself."

Maureen said that the Archangel Michael had come forward to speak with Jesus. He thanked the Lord for being with us and told Him how honored the angels felt to be in His presence.

Jesus replied, "You and the other angels are good servants who do God's will in an exceptional way." Michael smiled. I smiled.

"Lord, thank you for changing my boss's attitude toward me," I said. I had been a temporary secretary for her last year and had found her to be horrible to work for!

Jesus said, "Her being nice to you is tangible proof that you are being protected. Send loving thoughts to her as her soul is in need."

Of course I will and continue to do so.

I said, "Lord, I have a question I have wanted to ask you for a long time. How do I address you? Jesus? Christ? Lord? I'm never sure if I'm doing it right and I don't want to offend you."

He replied, "You may call me anything you are comfortable with." I was reassured by His words. I've always thought of Him as Jesus or Lord.

Jesus told Maureen and me that we were healers with Him in Biblical times. Both Maureen and I knew that we had had previous lives as healers with Jesus but this was the first time that we heard that the three of us had healed together.

I asked, "Were Maureen and I disciples?"

Christ replied "There were healers who also followed Me around the countryside. You were followers who assisted with the crowds following Me.:

Maureen and I looked at each other in wonder.

Jesus said that Maureen and I are beginning to remember our past relationships with him. This would explain our lack of surprise that He comes to us, and the special joy we feel inside when He does come.

I asked, "Lord, will I ever really be able to see You? I mean see what You look like and how You dress.

He replied, "Yes, you will. When you are ready."

That answer was like a two edged sword, why wasn't I ready now? But, I kept quiet. As happy as I am to know that I will be able to see Jesus and my other friends the way Maureen does I want it to happen immediately. I feel ready but who am I to argue?

We spoke about Mary's prophecies again. Jesus repeated, "The prophecies can be amended if people change their ways." He explained, "She [Mary] is Divine, I am Divine, each and every one of us is Divine. We are all one with God.

"The world needs love. We help others by showing love, healing and compassion."

We were quiet while I thought about all that the Lord had said. The light in my vision faded and I thought that He had left us. Maureen made a comment about how Jesus always wears those robes. That triggered a memory in me and I asked if Christ was still there. He came back and I asked if He was the robed figure seen by the Reiki Master who had given me my first Reiki attunement.

"Yes, it was I," was His reply. "I have always been there for you. Since you were a little girl I have been coming to you."

I wish that I had known! But, that triggered another memory. When I had had a Reiki healing with my former Master, she thought she saw the Brotherhood. I believe it was actually Jesus she saw with us that day.

We spoke about this book. I asked, "Lord what do you think of our book?"

He replied, "It is coming along very well. Books on spirituality are needed. People are hungry for your story."

We spoke of how He wants the book to end but you will have to wait to read his answer.

Again, Jesus receded into the background. Maureen was treating my back and I was feeling exhilarated and relaxed at the same time. I remembered a conversation I had had with one of my co-workers. She had commented on a video she had seen about angels and I was looking forward to borrowing it. When she mentioned that she heard on the video that angels did not reincarnate, I disagreed. She repeated that only our guides had the ability to incarnate. Again I disagreed. Gabriel is my guardian angel and I knew that he had reincarnated. I was determined to ask him and tonight was my chance.

I asked Maureen if Gabriel was there. She concentrated and said that "Yes, he is with us."

I asked, "Gabriel, are you an angel?"

"Of course, I am," was his reply.

"I knew it!" I crowed.

Remembering past questions I had wanted to ask Gabriel, I decided that now was the time. "What is an Ascended Master?" I asked.

"Someone who has been through the school of hard knocks," he replied. "One who has agreed to follow a spiritual path to learn the lessons that need to be learned. One who has become exalted to a high spiritual degree, ascended in a hierarchy of spiritual beings. One with the Light. One who has chosen specific lessons to be learned and has achieved it. Mastery through many incarnations."

"Am I an Ascended Master, too?"

"No, not yet."

I said, "I must still be going through the school of hard knocks."

Laughing, he replied, "Yes."

Thinking of Gabriel's costume, I wondered what I looked like in spirit form so I asked.

Gabriel replied, "To be here on earth, all spiritual beings have agreed to be in physical form. Spirit has no form, only the human form assigned to it. Molecular matter has no shape or form. It's one's imagination. Collectively, earth plane humans have assigned certain physical form and features to use as a descriptive.

"For example, a chair is a chair on earth because all agree that the form represents a chair. On other planes, that is not necessarily true. You humans create your own reality."

"Okaaayyy," I thought. "Not exactly the answer I was looking for but it is certainly a reminder to be more specific with my questions."

Maureen had worked her way down to my feet, which were sore. Interrupting the conversation, she asked, "Why are your feet hurting?"

I replied, "I don't know. I stopped wearing heels and have only worn flats for the last two weeks, but still my feet hurt at the end of the day."

Suddenly she said, "Your feet hurt because you are unconsciously holding back from the great and wonderful things that are waiting to happen to you."

"Really? Would you care to be more specific about that?"

"No. It will ruin the surprise."

I hate when she does that!

We thanked everyone for being there and ended the session. Once again, I had much to think about on the drive home. Mostly, though, I felt blessed.

A few days later, while we were doing our volunteer work at *Open Doors*, one of our clients didn't keep the appointment. Maureen and I decided to have a quick session and I lay on the table. Shortly after she began, Maureen whispered, "The big angel is here." Because there were other healers in the room, working with clients, we had to be very quiet so that we didn't disturb them.

"Let's find out who is he and what he's doing with us," I whispered back. It seemed important to me that we knew who this angel is as Maureen has seen him several times now.

"Who are you," I asked.

"Zechariah."

"Why are you so big?" I wanted to know. (Maureen had said that Zechariah often made himself as large as the entire healing room.)

"I make myself large to spread as much love as I can. The world needs much love."

Well, I certainly agreed with Zechariah. "What is your connection with us?" I wanted to know.

"I go before you to clear the way."

"Clear the way?" I asked.

"To help you accomplish your goals," he replied.

"Thank you. Thank you very much," I said gratefully. Unfortunately, we had to end our conversation as our next client had arrived.

A Visit with Pat

It will soon be time to say goodbye to our friend, Pat. The cancer in her lungs is progressing and all we can do is ease her pain and her breathing. Maureen had arranged for a group of volunteer healers to come in early to work with us as a team.

As always Pat was there promptly at the appointed hour. Another healer, Lisa, and I were the only ones there as yet. There had been an accident on the highway and traffic was backed up for miles. I decided that we would start anyhow and the others could jump in as they arrived.

I quickly got the table prepared and went out front to greet Pat. I explained that everyone hadn't arrived but Lisa and I were ready to start, the others could join in as soon as they could. As we walked back to the healing area, Pat told me that she was ready to die. She doesn't want to be here any longer.

Then she gave me a gift. Pat told me that she had been thinking of me a few days earlier. Her chest was hurting so she placed her hands on her chest the way that I do to channel healing energy into her. She said it didn't work but she tried.

Lisa and I began channeling energy into Pat. She was lying on the table, going to sleep when Maureen came and joined us. As the session went on, a total of eight healers had come to help Pat. With so much energy going into her for an hour, Pat was feeling very warm and understandably unsteady. I cooled her down as much as possible by giving her a drink of water and placing a cold cloth on the back of her neck.

After a few minutes, she got up and began hugging and thanking as many of the volunteers as she could (many were already working with clients and couldn't be interrupted). Maureen and I then escorted Pat outside to where her significant other was waiting. We told him to expect Pat to fall asleep and that she probably would not want to keep her appointment at 8:00pm that night.

Then Maureen and I went back inside. Since I did not have my own table that night, I decided to leave in order to arrange a surprise for my husband, David.

When Maureen and I spoke on the telephone the next day I asked if Pat had kept her scheduled appointment. Amazingly, she did. Maureen said that Pat's lungs were still pulling in a lot of energy but the rest of her body was fine.

Then Maureen told me that she had seen Jesus there, and that Pat saw Him as well. Maureen said that she saw Jesus pick Pat up and hold her in His arms, cradling her. The message to Maureen was that Pat would go soon and that she would go peacefully.

Later on, when Maureen told Pat what Jesus had said, Pat was happy to hear it. She has had enough. She said that she was ready to die. Pat threatened to stop having Reiki treatments because she felt that Reiki was the reason she was still alive. "Maybe if I stop having treatments, then I will be allowed to die. What am I staying around here for?"

"There is still something you must do." Maureen told her.

Frustrated, Pat asked, "What could be left? My affairs are in order. Everyone knows I'm dying. What else is there?"

"It is not for me to know," Maureen replied.

Helpless, there was nothing I could say or do. I thought about Pat's first Reiki experience. I was the healer assigned to work with Pat that night. She was a bit nervous because she did not know what to expect. Friends had recommended that she try Reiki and, deciding she had nothing to lose, came in.

I asked Pat, What can I do for you?"

She replied, "I have terminal lung cancer but that's not why I'm here. I'm having another, personal, problem that I want help with."

Maintaining my composure because I scarcely believed what she said, I told her to close her eyes and relax. I began.

At the end of the session, Pat was amazed at how great she felt. She hopped off the table and hugged me and asked, "How much money do you want?"

I replied, "I don't want any money, I'm a volunteer. You can put money in the donation basket at the front desk."

She insisted on giving me money and began stuffing money into my purse. After some discussion, I took money out of my purse and tried giving it back to her. Finally, I agreed to accept $10 while Pat agreed to put the rest of the money in the donation basket. I figured that after she left I'd put the $10 in the donation basket, as well.

The next day when I returned home from work, there was a very excited message on my answering machine from Pat telling me that the Reiki session had worked! David stood there listening and looked at me in surprise. It was the first time that he heard someone other than me say that Reiki worked. It was a bonus day all around.

"The Board"

Maureen and I were sitting on her living room couch, preparing to work on this book. I had removed Part One and refused to put it back in, despite David and Maureen's belief that I needed to keep the book intact. They believed it to be important. I believed that it would be hurtful to my family and as I have said previously, I don't like to talk about my past. It is too painful. I agreed to let Gabriel and Michael have their say before I made my final decision (which in my own mind was made but I wanted to be fair).

Maureen closed her eyes and immediately began to laugh. "They are all here and sitting at a large, crescent-shaped table, as if they are on a panel."

"Really?" I asked. "Who is here?"

"Gabriel, Michael, Jesus, Zechariah, and three others I don't recognize."

"Sounds like a board meeting to me!" I said.

Maureen looked at me and said, "I want to try an experiment with you. I will [silently] ask each 'board' member to come forward and I want you to identify him by the color that you see."

"All right," I agreed, surprised. "I'm ready to begin."

I closed my eyes and began to concentrate. Suddenly, my inner vision was filled with bright yellow. "That's how I see Zechariah. Am I correct?"

"Yes. Next?"

"I see a pale yellow. That's Michael. Correct?"

"Yes. Next?"

"I see Gabriel! He is always pale silver. And, Christ is always white and gold. He does not need to show himself to me. I always know when He is with us."

"Close your eyes and concentrate again. Can you see a rainbow of colors?"

I tried but to no avail. I opened my eyes and laughing, said, "I can't see a rainbow but the way my abilities have been developing, ask me again next week."

Maureen told me to once again close my eyes and concentrate. I did.

Suddenly, I was seeing red, green, blues and yellow. "I can see a rainbow! How did that happen?"

Maureen replied, "Each member of the Board is showing you his color. And, you didn't think you could do it!"

Well, I was tickled, but curious as to whom the remaining Board members were. So, I asked.

Jesus then introduced us to Saint Luke, Saint Mark and Saint Matthew, the remaining Board members.

"Lord, I am so honored. But, why are they here? I'm happy to meet them, but I am confused."

The Lord replied, "They, too, have written books that changed the world. They are here to help you."

"But, Lord," I protested. "These are great men who have done great work. My little book cannot compare to books in the Bible."

"If your book saves but one soul, isn't that good enough? If the book saves many souls all the better. You are like a candle in the darkness. Many people need to see your light."

"There are many lights out there, Lord. I'm in good company."

"Yes, this is true. But you are the one who is sharing her life with the world. You are the one baring your soul and are willing to be judged by people great and small. People need to read your story. Your entire story."

"But, Lord. The first part of my book is hurtful to me and I'm afraid of the hurt I may cause my family when they read it. I cannot, in good conscience, purposely cause them pain. It's not right."

"My child, eighty percent of the human population can relate to your life for parts will mirror their own lives. By reading the book, they will be able to see that they are not alone in their pain. They will see that no matter what they have done in their lives and to their lives, that they are loved by God the Father, by Me, and by many others in our realm. You will show them the way to the light by example.

"And, you are fulfilling your soul's destiny. Before you were born into this lifetime you agreed to be one of Our messengers by writing this book. You have free will and can refuse to write or publish this book. What will you do?"

I thought of my fears for I had several when thinking of writing and publishing my life story. I was afraid of causing conflicts within my family. I was very afraid of being called a fanatic and to be ridiculed by my family, friends and strangers. I was afraid for my soul if I didn't write this book. And, I was afraid of disappointing Jesus and the others. It was time to decide which fear was greater. I stalled to give myself time to think.

I looked out the picture window behind me and noticed what a beautiful day it was. The sky was a brilliant blue and the sun was shining so brightly that the outline of the trees stood out in stark beauty. I wondered if the Lord and others could appreciate the beauty the way we can. Still looking out the window, I asked my question.

Jesus replied, "Yes, child, we can. Thank you for asking."

Having reached my decision, I looked back to where I felt the Board was seated. "My soul agreed to write a book? My soul agreed to be one of God's messengers? How can I refuse? Lord, it will be done as you say. I will put Part One back in. I will get the book published. If I must choose between fear of what others will think and say about the book versus disappointing You, I will choose fear. For now I know that when

I am afraid to stand up as God's messenger, You will stand behind me and keep me steady. It doesn't take away the fear, but it will be easier to bear. Thank you."

"We are always there for you and always will be."

"I count on it, Lord. What do you think of the book? Do you like the work we have done so far?"

"We are very pleased."

The Board meeting ended at that point. While Gabriel, Michael and Zechariah remained with us, the others left. Maureen and I looked at each other, knowing we were now committed to seeing this book written and published in its entirety.

God has given us a wonderful gift: freedom. We have the gift to choose how we will live our lives. It's what we do with that choice that determines the outcome of our life. Everyone has two choices: to live a life which brings us closer to our soul's purpose, or to live a life that takes us away from our soul's purpose. At what point in our lives do we decide which will be our choice? Every minute of every day.

We are constantly making decisions and with each decision to be made, we have the choice as to how we will decide. For example, a cashier gives you an extra $5 when (s)he returns your change. You have a decision to make. Will you return the $5 or will you keep it, telling yourself that it's his/her problem. How do you think God would answer that question? Your response should be the same.

Jesus gave me this message to give to you: "People need to know that there is much help for them in our world and that it is most important that they weigh their choices and decisions carefully. For each decision brings with it the responsibility of accepting the consequences of their decisions. But more importantly, the only thing that is real is that humans just love one another (friend and foe, loved one and stranger) as a revered, sacred, honored soul. Master says, 'love one another as I have loved you.'"

Gabriel said, "Humans must know that when they make choices, they must be ready for the consequences. Think from the heart, not the head, from love not reactions. Don't make decisions from reactions, think 'what would the Lord do? How would Christ solve the problem?' Humans must realize that they are responsible for setting into motion the consequences of their actions. They have to understand that thoughts are capable of manifesting reality and that negative thoughts that are sent out to harm another, the thoughts that are cruel, do as much harm to their own spirit as if it was a physical assault. All thought has a reaction and a consequence. It is of most importance that humans understand the negative, as well as the positive, before sending a thought out to form reality."

"Is this the Debt of Karma?" I asked.

"Thoughtless reactions are to be avoided," I was told.

MEDITATION

God has chosen me to be one of his many messengers. What do you think is God's purpose for you? You have one, you know. You should begin to work to get in touch with your own team of angels. They will help you to discover your life's purpose. You must be patient. It may take quite a while to be able to hear and see your angels but continue to try. Think of it as your personal pot of gold at the end of the rainbow. You have to work at it but just look at your reward. To be able to hear what your own personal "spokesangel" has to say to you is truly wondrous. Speaking for myself, Gabriel has a voice the likes of which I have never heard before. It is soft and sweet, filled with love. You will thrill at the sound of hearing your angel's voice.

Meditation is one key to hearing your spokesangel. You really should meditate. Like most others, I found meditation to be difficult at first. Sometimes it takes 20-30 minutes for my mind to stop racing and quiet down, to be in the proper listening state. To me, meditation began as a way to relieve stress. Since I didn't feel that it was quiet enough, for long enough, to meditate at home I joined a group of people gathered specifically to mediate. I realized that I felt calmer after meditating and I was better equipped to handle daily stress. The big surprise for me was that David noticed the difference. I was quite taken aback one day when he asked if I was going to my meditation class.

"No," I replied, "It's snowing too hard for me to be driving such a long distance."

"Well, perhaps the weather will clear in time for your class. I don't like it when you don't meditate. I like you much better after you have attended your class. You aren't as tense all the time if you have meditated."

Well, if that wasn't a wakeup call, I don't know what one is! Now my meditations have two goals: to relax and work to connect with Gabriel and any other interested angels and guides. Of course, the connections do not happen unless I'm relaxed. I have been meditating long enough now that I can handle small household noises without feeling disturbed. And, it helps that my husband now works to keep things quieter for me since it benefits us both for me to get relaxed enough to meditate. I recommend to you: practice, practice, and more practice.

I realize that many people believe that meditation can only be done sitting on the floor in the lotus position. Wrong! Here is how I meditate: I set aside one hour to meditate. I find that this works best for me. Sit openly, even if you are not in the lotus position. For those of us no longer very nimble, sit in an armchair and rest your elbows on the armrests with palms up and head resting against the back of the chair. I rest my feet on a footstool and find this position to be very comfortable and relaxing. I play the same CD every time I meditate and burn the same candle. I find doing these things helps to put me in a meditative state more quickly. Naturally finding music and candle scent that resonates in you is vitally important. But no matter how you choose to sit, don't cross your legs one over the other or sit with your arms close to your body. Be open. This will make you more receptive. Close your eyes, take a few deep breaths and clear your mind (no matter how long it takes!). When random thoughts enter, just let them pass through, don't dwell on them and keep working to clear your mind. (This will take some practice.) Call your angels and guides to you. Tell them you are waiting to hear their messages. Don't be discouraged if nothing happens right away. I don't imagine there are many people on this planet who were able to place themselves in a meditative state without lots of practice. Keep at it. Mother Mary says that we should pray and meditate daily. Only you can judge how much time you can spare each day. Just don't give up. I've been meditating for over one year now and still am working to remove the blocks that keep me from hearing the sound of Gabriel's voice whenever I want to hear it. Sometimes it feels as if my ear is full, as if he is trying to talk to me but can't break through. You may not have blocks and may have a faster response rate than I do. Meanwhile, I look forward to the day I can have a conversation with Jesus, Gabriel and the others without assistance. That will be a time to treasure!

Ask your questions and quietly wait for an answer. You may not hear it in your ear but rather feel the answer. Or you may feel compelled to do or say something that would result in receiving your answer.

After meditating, I find that I am very relaxed and can easily go to sleep. If I am to meditate in the morning, it is before my shower or I won't want to be productive until after I nap. I'm too relaxed. A shower usually perks me up. When I meditate at night, I sleep like a baby.

And I always try to remember to thank my angels and guides for being there for me.

It doesn't matter whether you sit in a chair or do the lotus position or whatever works for you. It's making the connection to God and your angels that matters. I don't recommend lying down as you may fall asleep and that would seem to defeat the purpose of meditating. Just find which position suits you and DO IT!

GOD'S MESSENGER

People are afraid to believe that angels want to talk to me. I actually had a friend tell me that my hearing voices could be a sign that I am losing my mind. She is a dear friend and I was shocked by what she was saying to me. Instead of feeling the wonder that I expected her to feel, she was afraid I was going insane. She also drove home the point that people are afraid to step out of their boundaries, to let go of their long held beliefs. I feel sorry for them. They need to broaden their horizons.

You need to realize that angels are there for you, too. I'm not special and neither is Maureen. We're two sinners who got lucky. We saw what our lives had been like and decided to make the necessary changes in our lives. We cannot be the healers that we are if we didn't believe in God and all that believing in Him means. And anyone who doesn't think they can connect with God, whenever they want, is only fooling himself. God is there for everyone, no matter what you have done in your life. The secret is to believe that God is there, really there. And you must believe it and live it every minute of every day.

How many times during the day do you send a thank you to God? Do you thank Him for your life? For your day, no matter how difficult it was? Do you say thank you because you got all green lights one day when you were in a hurry? Do you say thank you for the food you have to eat? Yes? When was the last time you said thank you for having a great idea? Do you thank God when you see a beautiful sunrise or sunset? Or do you only thank God when a crisis is averted?

How many times in your life did you say "Oh, my God! Thank you, thank you, thank you" because that car that nearly sideswiped you missed you by an inch? Or the ever popular, "Please, God, if you give me _____, I'll never _____ again." Come on, admit it. How many times have you tried to bribe God with promises of being good if he grants your request?

When was the last time you invited God into your life? He would really like to hear that! Would it surprise you to know that I now ask God to be part of my life every day? I do it as soon as I remember—whether I'm in the shower, watching the morning news, or driving to work. The timing doesn't matter, doing it matters. Perhaps one day, I'll remember to invite God to share my day the moment I wake up. But, like everything else it takes practice.

Another thing that takes practice is letting go of your fear. So many books tell you to give your problems to God. That if you do that, all will be well. Well, that's certainly easier said than done. I know. I have failed God and myself many times with that stumbling block. But, if you believe strongly enough, and try it often enough, it works. And, all *will* be well. He still loves me no matter how often I have failed or disappointed Him. Just as He loves you.

Case in point. I had been working at a job that had so much potential for me. I was very excited to be paid a lot of money ("a lot" being relative), and working with a group of people whose mission was one I admired a great deal. For the most part, the people I worked with were very nice people. I felt very lucky, indeed. I worked hard and tried my best. But, for the first time in my professional life, my best wasn't good enough. Nothing I did was right as far as my manager was concerned. Nor was I a mind reader—a requirement that was left out of the job description. And, when my manager was in need of a scapegoat to vent upon, guess who the target was.

I became very depressed. I cried often, gained weight (yes, I'm one of those who eats when I'm depressed), was tired all the time, and felt as if

I was a failure. I was devastated and God was far from my mind. I prayed occasionally but didn't talk to Him. I thought we had a close personal relationship at this point and that I didn't need to get into all the details. I thought he already knew them. Well, he did know but since I couldn't let go of my problem, I didn't allow God to fix it.

By then, Gabriel and my Spirit Guides had had enough. The message came through to get out of that job, whatever it took. I was surprised but agreed to give my two-week notice. But when the time came I couldn't do it. I came close but decided the best thing for me to do was to wait until my contract expired in two months. Then I would leave. In my mind, it was a condition I could live with and still honor God's wishes. It wasn't exactly what I was supposed to do but it was the best way for me.

With the decision made, I put my situation into God's hands. My attitude changed drastically and I began to feel like my old self again. I could take whatever happened on the job and let it just slide away. If things didn't go smoothly I began to shrug it off. I was confident that I was no longer alone and God was my buffer. I began to smile again and make jokes with my co-workers. And, I began to write this book.

Shortly after making this momentous decision, I discovered that I was expected to invite God into my life every day. So every morning, I did. After a while, I realized, I was no longer intimated by my boss. I began to see her as just another human being who had her own doubts and fears to contend with. And it was becoming clear to me that while I knew that God was protecting me, she didn't seem to realize that God was working with her because she was still having a difficult time. I became relaxed and confident and was beginning to look forward to my last day of work. Almost as if God was giving me a reward for giving Him my problem, my manager began to treat me differently, too. Giving God my problem was the best decision I could have made.

And, as I invite God into my life every morning, every night when I pray, I thank Him for my day; for my life; for Jesus, Gabriel, Michael, and Zechariah; for my husband, daughter, grandson, and Maureen; my home, my family, my friends, my dogs, my job and for blessing me with a wonderful life. I pray for peace to be in our world. I ask God to help those who are sick and/or in need and finally, most importantly, I ask God to forgive me for whatever wrong I had committed that day. (Not being judgmental is very difficult for me. I often have to work on that.)

And you can't blame God when things don't go your way. You have to accept the blame for yourself no matter how difficult that is. And, believe me, I know how difficult it can be.

We all have lessons to learn. I try to identify them as I go through my day. For example, if I am driving along and I find myself behind a slow driver, I try to remember not to curse my bad luck. I try to think of it as a lesson in patience, something I'm short of no matter how many times my mother told me "Patience is a virtue."

Meanwhile, I've learned many lessons over this past year: how to make people feel better through my healing work; that I have a team of angels who love me no matter what I've done with, and to, my life; that God and Jesus believe in me and have faith in me; how to be kinder to others; the way I think about life and the people in it; how much more I appreciate what I have; and, how to be a better person. I imagine that as my journey continues, there will be many more lessons to be learned. And, I never forget Jesus telling me that I have many more trials to overcome in this life. Now that I know that the trials will improve me as a spiritual being, they will be easier to bear.

There may be other, more difficult lessons for each of us to learn. One difficult lesson to learn, for example, is the unexpected death of a loved one. Or perhaps in the birth of a child born with a birth defect. In our anguish, we cry, "Why God, Why? How could you do this to me?"

The only answer that I can offer is patience. I do not intend to undermine your grief as I, too, would grieve. But when your grief has eased I want to you to keep in mind that in this life we do not remember what lessons we need to learn for our soul to progress. We do not remember what arrangements we have made with other souls who have agreed to assist us in our heavenly progression. Nor do we know what lessons those we love must learn for their soul's progression. The good and bad experiences we have are to teach us the lessons our soul has agreed to learn. I believe that when tragedy strikes there are lessons for all involved to learn. How we deal with life's difficulties depends upon whether or not we will learn the needed lesson. We have the choice to decide how we will deal with life's emergencies and trials. Some people learn and continue on, while others shut themselves away, becoming bitter and hating life. We, as people, must decide how to handle the life our soul has chosen because a lesson our soul needs to learn has been given to us.

A family friend has recently become paralyzed due to a motorcycle accident. When I joined other family members visiting him in the hospital I was amazed at his acceptance of his new life. His sense of humor remained intact! His biggest concerns were how he was going to move around in the wheelchair when stairs would impede his progress and when could he return to work. Instead of feeling sorry for himself, he joked with us in the gentle way he always had. He comforted his fiancé because she is having a difficult time adjusting to their new lives. When he discovered that his neighbors were planning to build ramps at their home and to screen in the deck he had just enlarged, he had tears of gratitude in his eyes. He has no need for our tears and sympathy. He needs and accepts our love and returns it in full measure. He is a shining example to all who know and love him. Despite his paralysis, he is still the same loving man he always has been. It is obvious that he has accepted the dramatic change in his life. Unconsciously, he has chosen to accept the lessons his soul needs to learn and because of this, his acceptance will be a shining example to all who meet him. His is a light that burns brightly in the dark sky. Despite our misgivings and fear, he has chosen to become a beacon of hope to all who know him.

Another example of free will is to make the decision to become a more loving person. Remember the old saying, "Love thy enemy?" The angels want you to remember that what you reap so shall you sow.

The Archangel Michael reminded me of a lesson that I must learn. "Let go of expectations. As you are opening up spiritually and hearing messages, ask for clarity, identification and detailed information as you need it. You need to learn this lesson. You need to be more open with less definitive ideas as to what and how things should be. Gifts are given to all freely but each person must accept the gift in different ways. For example, the aura surrounding each person is there all the time whether you choose to see it or not. Each gift of knowing, gifts of the five senses are given specifically to use that gift in that framework. Just as some are gifted with painting while others are gifted with music. It is the same with spiritual gifts."

Michael's comments addressed my frustration in not being capable of hearing and seeing Jesus and His angels. I have been told that I have these gifts and my attitude of "well, what's taking so long!" apparently needed to be addressed. As a result of Michael's comments, I wrote myself a reminder that you may find useful in easing your frustrations: "Let go of expectations. Remember who leads the dance."

What lessons do you need to learn in this lifetime?

WHERE IS THE LOVE?

In *Mary's Message to the World*, we are told what will happen to this planet if we do not bring God and love into our daily lives.

I met a woman, 28 years old, did not end the conversation when I said that I was writing a book on my spiritual journey. Instead, she sought reassurance that the world was not going to end at the stroke of midnight January 1, 2000. I felt confident enough to reassure her that God did not have that particular date in mind. Or did she think that the Y2K bug was one of God's jokes?

I reminded her that after God destroyed the world, with the exception of Noah's Ark, He promised that He would never do that again. *Mary's Message* does not state that the world will end (meaning that the planet is not about to be blasted out of the galaxy) but that the world, as we know it, will end. In His visits to me, Jesus consistently repeats the message that in order to prevent Mary's prophecies from becoming realities, we must bring love into our daily lives. Love is what will save our planet.

"So now I am giving you a new commandment: Love each other. Just as I have loved you, you should love each other."

Jesus to his disciples at The Last Supper
John 14:34

And, then I watch the evening news and see how much hatred and strife is in the world. It frightens me. I'm worried that the people of this planet won't care what God desires. If I am to be a messenger of God, then I want the people of the world to hear Jesus' message of love.

He wants the people of the United States to set aside racism, discrimination, and hate.

He wants the Catholics and Protestants in Ireland to learn to stop hating each other and find a common ground so that healing and love can begin.

He wants the Serbs and the Albanians to find a way to live in peace in Kosovo.

He wants the North and South Koreans to learn to live as loving neighbors.

The Dalai Lama certainly wants the Chinese to leave Tibet alone. So does Jesus.

He wants the Indians and Pakistanis to stop fighting.

He wants the people of the Middle East to come together in peace, at last.

Wherever there is trouble and hatred, Jesus wants it to end. He wants people to remember that we are born to find love in our hearts. Can you find the love in yours? Your soul's greatest desire is to be a loving human being. Are *you* up to the challenge of becoming a loving human being?

I want the people of the world to remember the debt of karma. Think about this: if you are someone who persecutes those with different opinions, skin color, religion, etc.—watch out. In order to pay that debt of Karma, your next incarnation may well place you in the position of being the one persecuted to pay for the sins of your previous life. Remember what they say about payback?

I want all the people of the planet to hear Mother Mary's prophecies and take heed. I want them to know the jeopardy our planet and our lives are in if they don't find the love in their hearts.

The majority of humans are good and kind people, who for some reason have learned to hate another member of the human race. For we are each of us human and those with prejudice and hate in their hearts seem to forget that simple fact. We are all hurt by the cruel words of another; we all bleed red blood when we're cut or shot; and, we believe in God. For when we are in trouble whom do we call on for help? God.

One God with many children.

Each religion has wonderful men and women who helped to create the religion they believe in. But all those men and women worshipped by so many all bend their heads in prayer to the same God. One God.

It doesn't matter if we are Buddhist, Catholic, Hindi, Islamic, Jewish, Muslim, Protestant…or agnostic or atheist. God loves us. Jesus loves us. Our angels love us. No matter what we do. No matter how awful we are. No matter what our skin color is. No matter what country we were born in. No matter what religion we practice or don't practice.

And, yet, we do not love each other. How much pain and sorrow we cause those who love us most.

People look for Utopia never realizing that we each create our own—through love. Love of self and love of our fellow humans. What can we do to find the love buried beneath the hate? Dig deep into your soul and pray for God's help. Ask God, Jesus, Mary and your own personal team of angels to help you see the person you hate as a child of God—just like you.

Imagine a world where the evening news doesn't upset or depress you. A world where all people, of all nations, races, and religions are united in love of God and each other. Sounds Utopian to me.

For Jesus said, "Only love can save the world. With love the prophecies can change—the world can be saved."

Jesus also reminded me, "God is the way, the truth and the light." I think that this is a good lesson to remember.

I don't know about you, but I'll take Utopia.

EPILOGUE

Life is a roller coaster ride of good times and bad. Look at what has transpired in my life during the last twelve days:

- My husband, David, accepted a temporary (eight month) assignment in Chicago—1,500 miles away. He left 10 days ago. I'm alone again.

- My daughter, Lisa, is ill and so far the doctors haven't been able to determine the cause.

- My best friend's mother has cancer and has just arrived in Massachusetts for treatment.

- A family friend of thirty plus years has passed away

- My daughter and her significant other have ended their four-year relationship, with daddy getting custody of my grandson, Devin.

- My best friend's youngest brother, 35 years old, has died suddenly and for unknown cause.

- My sister-in-law's grandfather passed away.

- My mother is coming for a visit. Normally, a happy occasion but she hasn't read this book yet and I know that it will not be an easy read for her.

- And, our dear friend, Pat, has passed away.

Yet, I'm calm.

Before I learned so many lessons from Jesus, Gabriel and Michael, I would have been a nervous wreck worrying about how so many people were going to cope with their problems; but I'm not. I have, thankfully, learned my lessons well. These problems are in God's hands. I cannot live anyone else's life for them nor can I take responsibility for their problems.

I can only empathize.

No one needs my sympathy or criticism. What is needed is my strength, unconditional love and compassion—all of which I give gladly. After all, they were always there for me when I was in need. I can do no less for them.

I will never again forget that each of us has our own life to live, our own lessons to be learned, and our own mission from God. Who am I to interfere with that?

Love and light on your journey,
Linda Routhier

Afterword

Here I Am, Lord

I, the Lord of sea and sky, I have heard my people cry.
All who dwell in dark and sin My hand will save.
I, who made the stars of night, I will make their darkness bright.
Who will bear my light to them? Whom shall I send?

Here I am, Lord. Is it I, Lord? I have heard you calling in the night.
I will go, Lord, if you lead me. I will hold your people in my heart.

I, the Lord of snow and rain, I have borne my people's pain.
I have wept for love of them. They turn away.
I will break their hearts of stone, Give them hearts for love alone.
I will speak my word to them. Whom shall I send?

Here I am, Lord. Is it I, Lord? I have heard you calling in the night.
I will go, Lord, if you lead me. I will hold your people in my heart.

I, the Lord of wind and flame, I will tend the poor and lame.
I will set a feast for them. My hand will save.
Finest bread I will provide, Till their hearts be satisfied.
I will give my life for them. Whom shall I send?

Here I am, Lord. Is it I, Lord? I have heard you calling in the night.
I will go, Lord, if you need me. I will hold your people in my heart.

Dan Schutte

In memory of Pat Cloonen, God's messenger,
special to Jesus, friend.

Namaste (I honor your sacredness)

Reach out with your heart,
With peace, wisdom, and truth,
And with a clear inner voice you may say,

"I send you love."

"To the one in pain.
I send you love."

"To the desperate one with no vision,
I send you love."

"To the one that would hurt you,
I send you love."

"Send Love to All
And Love will greet you."

"Energy is a circle
It returns to you."

"Namaste."

By Karyn Mitchell

APPENDIX

Appendix A

Chakras are the primary conductors of energy within and without the human energy system. This energy system includes seven (7) major chakras. They are listed below.

1. The Root Chakra is located at the base of the spine and is generally thought to affect the circulatory system, the reproductive system and the functions of the lower extremities. The color most associated with the root chakra is red.

2. The Spleen, or Belly, Chakra is located in the lower abdomen. It is tied to the function of the adrenal glands and is an influence on the reproductive system as well as the entire muscular system. It influences the body's detoxification. This chakra is associated with the color orange.

3. The Solar Plexus Chakra is located where you would expect, the solar plexus, which is linked to the digestive system, the adrenals, stomach, liver and gall bladder. The color yellow resonates in the solar plexus.

4. The Heart Chakra is located between the breasts. It is tied to the function of the thymus gland and the entire immune system. It is linked to the right side of our brain and its processes. Green and Pink are the colors associated with the heart chakra.

5. The Throat Chakra is located at the base of the neck. It is tied to all the functions of the throat, esophagus, mouth and teeth, thyroid and parathyroid glands. The chakra corresponds with the color blue.

6. The Brow Chakra is located in the center of the forehead. It influences the functions of the pituitary gland and the entire endocrine system. It is also linked to the sinuses, eyes, ears, and face. The color indigo is associated with the brow chakra.

7. The Crown Chakra is located at the top of the head, or crown. It is linked to the functions of the nervous system as well as the skeletal system. It influences the pineal gland, all nerve pathways and electrical synapses within the body. The color violet is most associated with the crown chakra.

There are many more aspects to the chakra system as well as many books on the subject.

Appendix B

Wanting to know more about our angels, Maureen purchased the book, *Encyclopedia of Angels*. Listed below are brief descriptions of the angels described in *One Soul's Journey*.

Gabriel (God is My Strength): One of the seven archangels. He is one of the two highest-ranking angels in Judaism, Christianity, and Islam. He is best known for bringing important announcements to mankind. In the New Testament he announces the birth of John the Baptist to Zechariah (Luke 1:11-22) and the birth of Jesus to Mary (Luke 1:26-33). In Islam, Gabriel is called Jibril. It was Jibril who revealed the Koran to Muhammad. For this reason he is also called the faithful spirit, the faithful servant, and the bringer of good news. He is also the guardian angel of Muhammad.

Gabriella: The female form of Gabriel. In Judaic lore, Gabriel is believed to be a female angel, the only female in the archangel class.

Jesus: In Judaism he is a prophet. In Christianity he is the Son of God. In Islam he is called Isa and is also a prophet. The angels are said to have had no prior knowledge of the incarnation and the death of Jesus. His being born into the world and the events that followed during his time on earth are as extraordinary to them as they are to humans.

John the Baptist: A biblical prophet. John the Baptist was a cousin of Jesus Christ. He was also the messenger chosen by God to prepare the way for Jesus and is called the "forerunner" of Jesus. John's birth was foretold by the Archangel Gabriel who appeared to his father, Zechariah, to inform him that he and his wife, Elizabeth, would have a son.

Michael (Who Is As God): One of the seven archangels. He is God's warrior who leads the Celestial Army, and the ruler of the Seventh Heaven. The bible tells us that Michael and his army defeated Satan and his angels in the war in heaven, throwing them out of heaven and down to the earth. According to Judaic lore, it was Michael who prevented Abraham from sacrificing his son Isaac. Legend has it that it was also Michael who appeared to Moses in the burning bush. In Islam, Michael is called Mikhail. In the Koran the Cherubim are created from the tears of Mikhail.

Mikhail: One of the four archangels of Islam. It is the Islamic name for the Archangel Michael. In Islam, Mikhail is the angel "who provides men with food and knowledge."

Zechariah: See John the Baptist.

Suggested Reading

Conversations with God, An Uncommon Dialog (Book 1) by Neale Donald Walsh, G.P. Putnam's Sons, New York, NY 1996.

Conversations with God, An Uncommon Dialog (Book 2) by Neale Donald Walsh, Hampton Roads Publishing Company, Charlottesville, VA, 1997.

Conversations with God, An Uncommon Dialog (Book 3) by Neale Donald Walsh, Hampton Roads Publishing Company, Charlottesville, VA, 1998.

Essential Reiki, A Complete Guide To An Ancient Healing Art, by Diane Stein, The Crossing Press, Freedom, CA, 1995.

Mary's Message To The World, by Annie Kirkwood, Berkley Publishing Group, New York, NY, 1996.

The Healer's Manual, A Beginner's Guide to Energy Therapies, by Ted Andrews, Llewellyn Publications, St. Paul, MN, 1997.

The Seat Of The Soul, by Gary Zukav, Fireside and Colophonâ of Simon and Schuster, Inc., New York, NY, 1990.

BIBLIOGRAPHY

The Encyclopedia of Angels, by Constance Victoria Briggs, Penguin Putnam, New York, NY, 1997

Essential Reiki, A Complete Guide To An Ancient Healing Art, by Diane Stein, The Crossing Press, Freedom, CA, 1995

The Healer's Manual, A Beginner's Guide to Energy Therapies, by Ted Andrews, Llewellyn Publications, St. Paul, MN, 1997

Mary's Message to the World, by Annie Kirkwood, Berkley Publishing Group, New York, NY, 1996

Whose Hands Are These? A Gifted Healer's Miraculous True Story, by Gene Egidio, Warner Books, New York, NY, 1997

About the Authors

Linda Routhier, RMT, is a Karuna Reiki Master and Teacher, lives in Southeastern Massachusetts with her husband, two dogs and a cat, not to mention her team of angels, teachers and guides. Linda may be contacted at: **routhierl@aol.com**.

Maureen Niak, BNS. CHT. RTM., is a Karuna Reiki Master and Teacher, Clinical Hypnotherapist and Intuitive Counselor. She is also a Pre-Surgical Healing Facilitator.

If you would like to find a Reiki professional in your area, visit the International Association of Reiki Professionals' website at www.iarp.org.